For Matthew
A cherished companion
in depth-related humor,

Julien

Animal Rights and Moral Philosophy

Animal Rights and Moral Philosophy

Julian H. Franklin

Columbia University Press • New York

Columbia University Press

Publishers Since 1893

New York   Chichester, West Sussex

Copyright © 2005 Columbia University Press

All rights reserved

Library of Congress Cataloging-in-Publication Data

Franklin, Julian H.

Animal rights and moral philosophy / Julian H. Franklin

p. cm.

Includes bibliographical references and index.

ISBN 0–231–13422–3 (cloth : alk. paper)

ISBN 0–231–50871–9 (E-book)

1. Animal rights—Moral and ethical aspects.

I. Title.

HV4708.F74   2005

179'.3—dc22   2004055121

Columbia University Press books are printed on

permanent and durable acid-free paper.

Printed in the United States of America

Designed by Lisa Hamm

c 10 9 8 7 6 5 4 3 2 1

In memory of Marty Fleisher

But for the sake of some little mouthful of flesh we deprive a soul of the sun and light, and of that proportion of life and time it had been born into the world to enjoy.

—Plutarch, *Moralia*, "The Eating of Animal Flesh," 1.4

Contents

Contents

Preface

My purpose in this book is to rework the theory of animal rights and suggest some new directions. By animal rights I do not mean a utilitarian theory of animal liberation in Peter Singer's sense. Despite the great debt we owe to Singer for inspiring the modern movement for animal rights, I believe his case for respecting animal interests is theoretically inadequate. Singer's argument for animal liberation is founded on utilitarianism, which fails as moral philosophy. In the opening chapter of this volume, I shall restate the standard critique of that position, and I shall also try to show that there are several important issues on which Singer cannot give non-human animals[1] the consideration they deserve.

There are of course a number of utilitarians, or theorists influenced by the utilitarian position, who have contributed thoughtful pieces along the lines laid down by Singer. But it is no part of my project in this book to provide a history of doctrines or even to supply an outline of that history in recent times. I have concentrated on Singer because he best represents the central tenets and applications of the position. I shall also deal with R.G. Frey as one utilitarian who is diametrically opposed to granting moral consideration to animals. A position like Frey's is rare among utilitarians. But his position is worth considering briefly, if only to show that utilitarianism cannot be pressed into the service of a "case against animals." The utilitarian doctrine is inexpugnably egalitarian in its fundamental outlook, and while Singer's argument is flawed, in my opinion, I will try to show that Frey's is incoherent.

As things now stand, the best argument for giving full respect to animals is *The Case for Animal Rights* by Tom Regan. The criterion of moral action here is not, as with Singer, an aggregate of pleasure or pain in which the individuals who make up that aggregate are mere receptacles of units of utility. For Regan, all mammals of a year or more in age have an inherent prima facie right to life and liberty. This is the main thesis of a powerful and sympathetic case for animal rights, and I shall consider it at length in chapter 2. As might be expected, there are a number of theorists who have adopted a similar approach, but once again I shall concentrate on Regan as the prime exemplar.

For all its virtues, the rights argument, as it is commonly understood, is incomplete. The system of reflective intuitions that lead to equal rights for animals is consistent, and in my opinion airtight. Those who criticize Regan for relying so much on intuition fail to consider adequately the imposing chain of his reflections. The real problem is rather that this superstructure lacks a solid base. Regan assumes, as universally granted, that animals cannot be treated "in just any way." This is a crucial assumption, but Regan does not attempt to justify it.

In chapter 3, I shall try to find a foundation for that judgment in Kant's categorical imperative. Kant, of course, is notoriously dismissive of rights for animals. He presents the categorical imperative as though it covers rational beings only. Taking Kant at his word, theorists of animal rights regularly pass his moral doctrine by. But this is a costly mistake. Kant confuses the subjects of the categorical imperative, which are and must be rational beings, with the objects to which the categorical imperative applies. I will try to diagnose this confusion, and after dealing with all three forms of Kant's categorical imperative, I will venture to conclude that their basic moral principle is properly rendered by the categorical imperative in a revised version of its second form. It should now be taken as though it reads as follows: *Act in such a way that you always treat sentience, whether in yourself or in the self of any other, never simply as a means but also at the same time as an end*.

Chapter 3 will also examine Evelyn B. Pluhar's alternative form of rationalist morality. Pluhar dismisses Kant. But she believes that a theory of animal rights can be derived from the rationalist ethic of Alan Gewirth. Although her effort is noble and ingenious, I will argue that it too is insufficient. It wholly depends on Gewirth's rationalist ethics, which will be criticized as unsustainable.

In chapter 4 I shall consider some of the best known attempts to preserve a Kantian viewpoint without directly relying on his moral theory. Rawls and Habermas, each in his own way, do not begin with an analysis of rationality as such. Instead, they presuppose a community of humans and ask for the rules of justice or morality that it will adopt under constraints requiring all of its members to respond reasonably to questions of justice and morality. These theories ignore the rights of animals more or less completely, and I shall try to show in chapter 4 that they do so only at the price of inner consistency. Here I will go back very briefly into history to show that my objections to Rawls and Habermas are adumbrated in Diderot's reflections on the idea of a general will. I will then end this chapter with a brief critique of the contractarian efforts of Jan Narveson and Peter Carruthers.

Chapter 5 deals with attempts to develop a theory of respect for animals from human feelings of compassion. These are moving efforts, and compassion can surely evoke and supplement the moral imperative derived from reason. But compassion, I believe, cannot stand alone as an independent basis of equal respect for animals. Without a foundation in reason it will always lack a proper basis of discrimination. I shall try to show this by a critique of two very prominent positions of this sort: Albert Schweitzer's "ethic of reverence for life" and the feminist, or ecofeminist, "ethic of care." At the end of the chapter, there are some very brief remarks in which I question whether equal respect for animals can be reached by appealing to religion.

The last chapter, on environmentalism and animal rights, seems to be a change of topic. But the use of nature is the main area in which human and animal rights conflict. By a conflict of rights, I mean situations wherein the *legitimate* interests of animals and the *legitimate* interests of humans directly clash. The eating of meat is not a clash between the animal and the human right to nourishment, since the animal is used as a mere instrument for human satisfactions. The same applies to the use of animals for biomedical experiments. This is not a conflict of otherwise legitimate interests. Animals alone are made to sacrifice; they do not give consent.

On the other hand, competition between humans and animals for the use of a particular natural resource is an authentic conflict of otherwise legitimate interests. This poses a dilemma to which I believe a reasonable solution can be found. The advocates of animal rights and hard-core ecologists are too often driven to extremes. Tom Regan and J. Baird Callicott are prime examples of this. I shall argue instead for a middle position. Humans have priority over animals, but only with an important limitation. Any new or more intense appropriation of nature must be justified by a clear showing that the general quality of human life will be advanced thereby and that no reasonable alternative exists.

I have also included an appendix on animal consciousness. Proponents of animal rights, somewhere in their discussion of the main issues, point out that Descartes and his modern heirs are mistaken in their claims that animals lack awareness and so do not feel pain, but I have not done so in the body of the text. Cartesianism in its modern form is so diametrically opposed to common sense, is so weak a case, and is so clearly entertained only by hard-core opponents of animal rights, that I have decided not to dignify it by inclusion as a chapter. After a brief comment on Descartes and his early followers, I shall take up, and I hope effectively refute, four representatives of modern neo-Cartesianism.

Except for the foray into environmentalism, I do not comment on questions of public policy. I try to focus solely on moral philosophy. Nevertheless, I feel bound to say something about the use of animals for biomedical experimentation. If the argument for animal rights is correct, this practice must be wrong. Yet many educated laymen, considering animal rights more or less for the first time, are appalled by this particular implication. I thus feel obliged to state, however briefly, how I stand on this issue. Since this is not properly within my topic, I will include my thoughts in a second brief appendix.

Acknowledgments

This book is philosophical. I plan to deal with certain major issues of moral philosophy as they apply to concern for animals. I have tried to arrive at a persuasive theory of animal rights, by which I mean the right of animals to be treated equally with humans so far as their interests are relevant. Animals obviously cannot have a right of free speech or a right to vote because they lack the relevant capacities. But their right to life and to be free of exploitation is no less fundamental than the corresponding right of humans.

My exploration of these questions comes late in my career. My academic specialty is the history of political thought, within which I have specialized in theories of absolutism and constitutionalism in the sixteenth and seventeenth centuries. But I have always had a very deep concern for animals and great revulsion for the ruthless ways in which they are exploited. I have long contributed to animal causes, and I have been a vegetarian (with vegan aspirations) for the last twenty years. After retiring from full-time teaching in 1996, I gradually became more active in behalf of animal rights. After a few years of searching, I settled on teaching and writing on animal issues.

I don't expect that many readers will be converted to the cause of animal rights by reading this book.

Indeed, the ability of intelligent and educated people to avoid confronting the issue, or to offer endless evasions and rationalizations of delay on a question as straightforward as vegetarianism, even when they have heard and (reluctantly) accepted the argument in favor, is astonishing as well as depressing. If they are to be swayed, the change is likely to come from witnessing the realities of the fate endured by animals. I have not reviewed these horrors here, because so many powerful accounts exist. Nor have I dealt with advances in the legal protection of animals both in practice and in theory. I have focused exclusively on moral theory.

Nevertheless, I believe that a good theoretical argument is worth the effort. It can reassure the committed, help the uncertain to decide, and arm the debater. There is a vital long-term benefit as well. If the idea of animal rights continues to be recognized intellectually, and if it grows in acceptance as a classroom subject, a good theory will help to solidify a cultural change toward greater concern for animals—a change that is already under way. I hope that this book will help this cause along.

The idea for a book on animal rights goes back to an undergraduate colloquium I gave at Columbia in the spring of 1999. But the central thought was shaped by a graduate course I taught at Rutgers University-Newark in the fall of 2000. I wish to thank Professor Mary Segers of Rutgers-Newark for arranging the invitation, and Professor Elizabeth Hull, who sat in on most of our meetings and whose support was invaluable. At the early stages of this work, discussions of Kant with Thomas Pogge played a vital role in clarifying my thought. And I was greatly encouraged to push on by Eileen Sullivan's thoughtful comments on that early set of reflections.

Cynthia Bowman, George Klosko, and Guenter Lewy helped me greatly by their critical reading and helpful comments on the full first draft. At various times I also got advice and encouragement from Robert Amdur, Abraham Ascher, Karen DeCrow, Solomon Goldstein, Istvan Hont, Francine Klagsbrun, Alex Kolben, and Frank Lovett. And I received a number of useful suggestions from the readers for Columbia University Press.

It was truly good fortune to have Wendy Lochner as my editor. She is the Senior Executive Editor for Religion, Philosophy, and Anthropology at the Columbia University Press, and she was thoroughly supportive and thoughtful throughout the complicated process that publishing a book requires.

Another piece of good fortune is that my wife, Paula, who is herself a retired book editor, did heroic service in editing the entire final draft before I turned it in. Not only was her copyediting superb, but she raised shrewd and helpful questions on points of substance. She also took over, unobtrusively, many of my usual household chores during the final dash to finishing.

Animal Rights and Moral Philosophy

1

Peter Singer
and Utilitarianism

The idea that humans have at least some obligations
to animals is very old. To varying degrees, it is found
in totemist taboos and ceremonies, in all developed
religions of the West as well as of the East, and among
notable philosophers of classical antiquity, including
Pythagoras, Theophrastus, Plutarch, and Porphyry.
Most of these doctrines are incomplete in that they
do not deal with all the issues that would now be taken
up in considering animal rights.

Some, like the Hebrew Bible's, concentrate solely
on cruelty to animals, while permitting the consumption of animal flesh and requiring animal sacrifice;
others, like Plutarch's and Porphyry's, deal mostly
with vegetarianism and temple sacrifices. None of
them, however, not even the classical philosophers,
systematically develop the obligations of humans to
animals from philosophical foundations. That deficiency is only now beginning to be rectified.

In modern times there are two mainstream positions in which the idea that animals are entitled to
equal respect with humans is systematically and
more or less comprehensively developed.

One of these is that of Peter Singer, who is the
leading exponent of utilitarianism as it applies to
respect for animals. I shall begin with Singer because

it is his book *Animal Liberation* that initiated the modern movement. Animal liberation, or animal rights, go beyond animal welfare and humanitarianism in its usual form.[1] Showing kindness to animals and protecting them from cruelty are good, but no longer enough. The revolutionary point in the idea of animal liberation is that animal interests must be accorded the same respect as that given to humans.

In its simplest form, utilitarianism holds that pain is the only evil and pleasure the only good, and that the test of whether an act is moral is whether its consequences, when all the pains and pleasures that the act causes to those affected by it are calculated and added up, produce the greatest aggregate of well-being or happiness as compared to any other course of action. Once we admit that all sentient beings can suffer pain and feel pleasure, they too must included in the reckoning. If animals no less than humans feel sensations, their pains and pleasures no less than ours must count.[2] That surely was the opinion of the founder of modern utilitarianism. "The day *may* come," says Jeremy Bentham,

> when the rest of the animal creation may acquire those rights which could never have been withholden from them but by the hand of tyranny. The French have already discovered that the blackness of the skin is no reason why a human being should be abandoned without redress to the caprice of a tormentor. It may come one day to be recognized, that the number of legs, the villosity of the skin, or the termination of the *os sacrum*, are reasons equally insufficient for abandoning a sensitive being to the same fate. What else is it that should trace the insuperable line? Is it the faculty of reason, or, perhaps, the faculty of discourse? But a full-grown horse or dog is beyond comparison a more rational, as well as a more conversable, animal, than an infant of a day, or a week, or even a month, old. But suppose the case were otherwise, what would it avail? the question is not, Can they *reason*? nor, Can they *talk*? but, Can they *suffer*?[3]

Bentham never followed this principle to its logical conclusion. He did not, for example, rule out the eating of animal flesh entirely, pleading only for humane methods in slaughtering. But the climate of general opinion was more favorable to larger considerations when Peter Singer took up the issue. Systematically pursuing more extensive possibilities, he began a whole new chapter in the movement for animal equality by radicalizing Bentham's suggestion. After exposing the horrors of factory farming and the callous waste of animal lives in biomedical testing and experimentation, he argues that the consumption of animal flesh under present circumstances is morally wrong. Wrong also, he insists, is biomedical experimentation at least as it is now practiced.[4] Singer has also been relentless in exposing the sophistries and fables that enable even allegedly sensitive and thoughtful people to go on with their speciesism (213ff.).[5]

It would seem that no serious utilitarian could doubt that animals have to be included in the calculation of aggregate happiness. Nevertheless, there is at least one utilitarian who has sought to do just that. R. G. Frey has dedicated much of his career as a philosopher to refuting claims of equal respect for animals. There is no need, he argues, for hungry humans to worry about sensations of pain in animals when considering their dietary preferences. Vegetarianism in all its forms is nonsense. Although an avowed utilitarian,[6] Frey nonetheless sees no difficulty arising in the conscience of a meat eater even if he or she is also a committed utilitarian consequentialist.

Merely eating the meat of animals, Frey argues, has nothing to do with actually killing them or causing them to suffer. The human carnivore, as he would have it, who merely buys and eats the meat, bears no responsibility for what the factory farmer or the butcher did:

> Suppose my neighbour shoots and kills a turkey: even if it was wrong of him to kill it, is it wrong for me to eat it? It is not obvious how the argument from killing (or the other arguments) can show that it is, when the person who does the eating is different from the person who does the killing, which is the case, of course, with meat we buy in the supermarket. After all, where killing or violating rights or inflicting suffering is concerned, it is normally the person who does these things who is morally suspect. And even if we allow that most abbatoirs would not exist if most people did not eat meat, it does not follow

that the wrongness of the slaughterer's act of killing, if it is wrong, somehow mystically transfers to the consumer's act of eating. It is true that animals are killed in order to be eaten; but it is killing, not eating, which carries the moral force in the argument from killing and which is being condemned.[7]

Strict utilitarians do not consider death an evil to the individual who suffers it so long as it is painless and unsuspected in advance, and Frey in this respect is strict. That is not only indicated in the above quotation, but is spelled out at length in a later chapter. Frey is well aware, of course, that the killing of animals as now practiced is inseparable from suffering, and he dispenses the diner from worry about that as well. But the decisive point in the passage quoted is the argument that the eater bears no responsibility for the death (and suffering) of the animal eaten. It is just not his or her concern.

I am baffled by Frey's reasoning. I do not understand how a utilitarian, or for that matter any moral person, can be indifferent to the consequences of his or her actions. Perhaps a homely parallel will illustrate my problem. A thief steals some jewels in an act that, let us agree, is wrong either because it is inherently wrong or because its consequences for society are bad. Now suppose I buy the jewels for resale, knowing they were stolen. Am I not guilty of encouraging a wrong by profiting from it? If I also let the thief know, by words or repeated purchase of successive hauls, that I am a good prospect for the disposition of his or her future thefts, am I not even more involved in his or her crime? And would I not have done wrongly, not only under statutory law but under moral law as well, and by any calculus of the utilities involved? How does the case of a meat eater differ from that of the jewelry fence? I am supposing, of course, that the diner in question has finally heard the news that the process of farming, transporting, and butchering animals is not exactly gentle and painless.

Frey also reflects that a single vegetarian would have only a negligible effect if he or she were acting all alone and had not achieved a large body of support for a boycott of meat by the eating public. Abbatoirs, he informs us, would not go out of business just because one person abstains. No doubt. But that abstention, continued over a period of time, would mean that sooner or later one less animal would live a painful life and die a painful death. Why does that not matter to a consequentialist? Frey also protests that there are ways of combating the suffering connected with meat eating other than vegetarianism. That too is undoubtedly true. But why not give up eating meat as well?

Frey would have us worry about the pain that would be suffered by all those humans who would lose their jobs and businesses if eating meat were widely abandoned.[8] It is not highly likely of course that this would happen so quickly that readjustments could not be planned and made. But suppose we grant that vegetarianism could supervene overnight. Even so, Frey, the utilitarian, would have no ground to put the blame upon the herbivores. For he has not yet done the necessary homework. Has Frey calculated, even roughly, the amount of pain caused to untold billions of animals yearly and weighed it against the possible future inconveniences that would be suffered in the course of reemploying people connected with the meat industry? And has he added in, on the side of vegetarianism, the vast increase in the productivity of agriculture that would be made possible by the elimination of large-scale animal husbandry, which is an extremely wasteful way of processing grain into food? A utilitarian could hardly ignore the increased well-being that could then result for the vast number of people worldwide who now suffer malnutrition.

I have raised these doubts about Frey mainly to underline my earlier remark that utilitarianism, correctly understood, is bound to take the suffering of animals seriously. I have enormous respect for the decency of that position and the good that it has done and still does on a great many moral issues.

Despite its heroic accomplishments, however, utilitarianism is flawed as a philosophic doctrine. It holds, against common sense, that killing is not an evil if the death is painless to the victim, if it does not set a bad example, and if it does not cause pain to those who cared about the deceased. It also holds, again in the face of common sense, that the aggregate well-being of a group may be raised by enlarging the number of its members, even though each individual is made worse off in the process. Thus, if everyone in a group had a utility index of 10 and there were 100 members, the aggregate utility of the group would be 1,000. But suppose that by lowering each individual's utility index to 8, we can increase the size of the group to 150. We now have an aggregate utility index of 1,200. Happiness, accordingly, reigns supreme in some abstract aggregate, but everyone has become worse off!

Some utilitarians would remove this embarrassment by substituting average utility for aggregate utility. Thus, in the example given, the first arrangement would be superior because the index of average utility is 10, not 8 as in the second. But now there is a new embarrassment. It follows that in any group with a range of indices—say a group of ten where the individual members have utilities ranging from 1 to 10 in order—the aggregate utility would be 55 and the average utility index is 5.5. Now let us suppose that we kill off (painlessly, of course) the member whose average utility index is the lowest, i.e., 1. The aggregate utility now goes down to 54, but the average utility index gains. It is now up to 6 and would continue to increase each time we kill off the member with the lowest index of utility. At the end, the average utility will go up to 10. But now the aggregate utility will drop down to 10 as well, and the membership of the group will now be just one member with a utility index of 10. Thus will average utility be maximized! The logical result of either criterion of utility is thus morally and ethically counterintuitive.

There is yet another set of objections to utilitarianism, arising from the need to calculate and compare amounts of pleasure. What constitutes a pleasure? Are some "better" than others in the sense of being "higher"? How are units of utility to be assigned absolutely to each pleasure of an individual in order to calculate the utility index of a given individual? And if that is not difficult enough, the difficulties become overwhelming when we have to compare the utility index of one individual with another's. All these calculations and comparisons are needed in order to get a reckoning of the consequences of an act, and the difficulties are the same whether one is interested in aggregates or averages of utility. Yet it is obvious that different people have different sensibilities that have no common denominator.

This last group of problems can be overcome by broad definitions and rough estimates. There is usually no need for mathematical precision in calculations of utility. But there is yet another difficulty with utilitarianism which I find most seriously at odds with common sense and moral intuition. This is the notorious inability of utilitarianism to introduce considerations of fairness into the distribution of pains and pleasures. Whether we are calculating the aggregate or average utility of a group, we will often—indeed almost always—have to sacrifice the interests of one or more innocent individuals in order to maximize the result we are seeking. Let us suppose that we again have a group of ten individuals each of whom has a utility index of 10. The aggregate utility will be 100 and the average utility 10. Now let us suppose that we can give three individuals (chosen impartially by lot) a utility index of 20 at the cost of reducing the utility indices of the remaining seven to 6. The aggregate utility will now go up to 102 and the average utility will rise as well, to 10.2. Each individual has been accorded equal respect in that there has been no discrimination. Yet if we are good utilitarians, we will sacrifice the interests of the six to the three in order to maximize utility. In the same fashion we can arrive at even more intense deprivation, imposing a very extreme sacrifice on a small minority to achieve a higher aggregate or average utility index from which only the majority benefit.

This is a result which we would intuitively call unjust. The utilitarian, however, cannot use that term. Unjust for the utilitarian is only what public legislation forbids by its commands. Apart from fear of the law, he or she is committed to maximizing the good, which, we have tried to show, has nothing to do with what we normally and intuitively call fairness. There is a value called justice which exists independently of maximizing utility. At the very least, it has to do with treating equally situated people equally.

Most of the criticisms made above have to do with act utilitarianism. In this version of the doctrine, its classical Benthamite form, the consequences of each act must be calculated. But various amendments of classical act utilitarianism have been suggested for evading or mitigating this defect. The most powerful of these is rule utilitarianism, which substitutes the overall utility of obeying a rule for the utility of each individual act. My theft of that watch over there may be justified by act utilitarianism since the owner, let us assume, will suffer less from losing it than I will gain by stealing it. But if I reflect that the rule against stealing benefits society in the long run, then I know that I must follow that rule in order to maximize utility. All or most of the rules of fairness may thus be salvaged as enhancing the aggregate utility.

The problem here is that the rule cannot, if founded strictly on utility, bind the individual actor if the act, even though against the rule, would increase overall utility if taken alone. Thus, in my particular circumstances paying one's taxes, for example, might not advance (and might even reduce) the aggregate utility of all. By the principle of Bentham's act utilitarianism, it would actually be wrong for me to pay. Yet the general rule that taxes should be paid will almost always advance well-being in the long run, if everyone observes it, and so I ought to pay out of consideration for the rule. But now suppose that I can avoid payment of my tax and not be detected, and suppose also that my evasion will advance not only my own but the overall utility when all the individual utilities and disutilities are aggregated. When I aggregate the deprivation I will undergo as an individual with the benefit to the public that would follow from paying my taxes, it may turn out that I could increase the aggregate utility of the whole society by not paying, unless, of course, I set a bad example to other folks who really ought to pay. Would it not, then, be my duty as a true utilitarian not to pay? For if I am able to hide the omission, I do not set a bad example and I maximize the aggregate of utility. But if I may, and indeed must, make that calculation, so must everybody else, and we are back to act utilitarianism. Rule utilitarianism, therefore, may be useful as a rule of thumb, i.e. it is usually better to pay. But in theory, rule utilitarianism collapses into act utilitarianism unless it introduces an extraneous element of obligation, i.e. that one is simply obliged to follow the established rule without calculating individual circumstances.

Singer, perhaps to his credit, is not deterred by the distributive paradoxes which arise from utility maximization. He simply follows the logic of utilitarianism to its end, issues of distributive justice notwithstanding. This is not nearly so difficult in practice as it may seem to be in the abstract. The outrageous results that utility permits in principle rarely come to pass. Thus slavery is technically permissible if it pays off in aggregate utility. But it rarely does. Utilitarians, therefore, are reluctant to give up a simple and powerful tool of ethical evaluation merely to avoid what are mostly hypothetical embarrassments.

There is, however, another question in utilitarianism that is much more immediately related to the issue of respect for animals. Is death a disutility in itself or is it evil only in the collateral pain or fear it causes others? Is the death of a human no more serious an evil than the death of an animal? The usual solution here is the doctrine of collateral effects. The death of a human may cause others to suffer from loss or fear for themselves, but the (painless) killing of a chicken or a cow usually does not.

Singer, however, prefers not to rely on something as secondary to the calculation of aggregate utility as peripheral effects, and turns instead to "preference utilitarianism" for a solution. Preference utilitarians hold that the element to be considered in measuring the well-being of an individual is not felt pleasure or pain, but rather the satisfaction or frustration of his or her preferences. Humans, endowed with self-consciousness as they are, can alone have a conscious preference for life as such. And so it is that humans, and humans only, suffer loss from death even if that death is painless. You can therefore kill a chicken if the death is painless, and there is no loss of aggregate utility from the act if you replace the chicken you have killed with another chicken having the same utility index. So to permit the killing of animals for food (under very special conditions of course) cannot be used to justify killing innocent humans and replacing them.

But the implications of preference utilitarianism as Singer invokes it notoriously do not end there. Infants, like chickens and coyotes, cannot be said to have a conscious preference for life. Infanticide, accordingly, is not only permissible if the infant killed is replaced by another with roughly the same utility index. It would often be mandatory in that replacement of a deformed child with a healthy one may be a gain in utility. Besides, a deformed child, if it is allowed to live, may not find positive utility in its future existence.[9]

There are numerous difficulties with preference utilitarianism, some of which seem fatal to the whole idea. We may begin with a practical absurdity. Along with a preference for life, an individual will have many desires for self-realization in the future. Are we pledged to honor these if the individual dies suddenly of a natural cause? Animals, furthermore, indicate a fear of death and a preference for life by their cries and behavior.[10] They surely moan when they are being led to slaughter, and this cannot simply be attributed to their fear of pain. Finally, consider that once a human individual is dead, it is extremely hard to understand how he or she can experience the disappointment of a preference for life now that the life is over. Another way of putting this difficulty is to ask why one entity with a preference for life may not be replaced by another entity which also has a roughly similar preference for life. And so, like chickens, like people!

In a rights approach to respect for animals, which we will take up in the next chapter, the main consideration is justice. Hence the theoretical differences between any version of utilitarianism and a rights approach are fundamental. But we are bound to note that the differences between someone like Tom Regan, the best known proponent of animal rights, and Singer do not always show up in their practical recommendations. For Regan, eating the flesh of animals clearly violates their rights, and Singer too arrives at a vegetarian position. There may be nothing wrong with eating meat if the animals are killed painlessly. But painless killing, Singer notes, is all but impossible to realize in practice. Where the number of consumers is large, some form of factory farming will inevitably be introduced to accommodate supply to the demand. In practice, therefore, a strict utilitarian may not eat meat.

One might also suppose that a utilitarian would justify eating meat if the cost to animals in suffering were less than the cost to human beings in foregoing the pleasures of the table and in economic dis-location. But given the vast number of animals who endure many kinds of pain before they suffer a painful death, aggregate utility, no less than the theory of rights, points to vegetarianism.

But on some points the differences between utilitarianism and a theory of animal rights are sharp, although not always spelled out. Utilitarianism cannot rule out various common forms of animal suf-fering that Singer, no less than a rights theorist, would presumably regard as cruel. Rodeos give much pleasure to a great number of peo-ple, so that the aggregate of pleasure for the humans is surely greater than the total of pain caused to relatively few animals. Much the same reasoning would remove the usual objection to zoos. And for all of his misgivings, Singer has to admit, however reluctantly, that experimentation on animals cannot be excluded altogether. He is bitterly opposed to what a utilitarian might call "a waste of pain," as when too many animals are used for too many useless experiments and tests, and he is quite right to hold that there ought to be much greater control over the treatment of laboratory animals if their use is to be legitimate.[11] But these are things on which all, or almost all, professional associations agree without challenging the practice of experimentation on animals as such. Singer also notoriously insists that mentally defective humans (who also have no loved ones who would suffer collaterally) can be used in experiments and tests as freely as higher mammals like primates. His purpose is to show that admitting such a possibility might lead to caution in experimenta-tion on animals generally.[12] But the point for our present purposes is that Singer is bound to admit that the cost in suffering inflicted on a small number of humanely housed animals by carefully designed experiments and clearly needed tests would be legitimate if the pain were indeed offset by reasonably expected benefits to other individ-uals, animal as well as human, from the useful knowledge thus acquired.

These limitations of utilitarianism cannot be circumvented. But even if they could be, the position would still be unacceptable. The case for animals ought not to be built on a philosophy whose basic principles are so inadequate.

2

Regan on Animal Rights

If utilitarianism is to be set aside as a doctrine of
respect for animals, the most likely alternative is a
theory of animal rights. Among modern moral
philosophers the first to advance such a theory systematically was Tom Regan. His rights position is
powerfully set out in *The Case for Animal Rights*,
which appeared in 1983.

Regan's starting point is a critique of Descartes
and certain neo-Cartesians[1] of the present time in
order to remove any lingering doubts that animals
are conscious and have feelings and that they may
also possess a significant degree of subjectivity.[2]
Regan is especially concerned with "normal mam-
malians, aged one or more." These are most like
human beings who have passed the stage of infancy:

> Individuals are subjects-of-a-life if they have beliefs
> and desires; perception, memory, and a sense of the
> future, including their own future; an emotional life
> together with feelings of pleasure and pain;
> preference- and welfare-interests; the ability to ini-
> tiate action in pursuit of their desires and goals; a
> psychophysical identity over time; and an individual
> welfare in the sense that their experiential life fares

ill or well for them, logically independently of their being the object of anyone else's interests.   (243)

There is of course a much larger range of beings that can feel pain and appreciate release therefrom.[3] Indeed, all beings that are sentient might well be considered. For the moment, however, that issue need not be resolved. No matter how the line is drawn, there will be many species of animals whose members have a strong claim to rights.

Regan's discussion of animal consciousness and related questions of what constitutes a satisfactory life for animals concludes with the critically important observation that "no serious moral thinker accepts the view that animals may be treated in just any way we please."[4] But this does not necessarily, or even normally, mean that all serious moral thinkers agree that animals have rights in the sense that we are directly obligated to respect them. In the grand philosophical tradition, thinkers who recognize a duty to animals believe this duty to be only "indirect." Regan takes up Jan Narveson's rational egoism,[5] John Rawls's contractualism, and Immanuel Kant's categorical imperative to illustrate this point of view. Narveson's rational egoism, Rawls's agreement in the original position, and the various forms of Kant's categorical imperative are designed to apply to humans only—to moral agents, as Regan puts it, who can act by understanding rules and making agreements, but not to animals or moral patients who cannot. But all the theorists mentioned agree that this rule could be detrimental to the interests of the human species. At least indirect consideration must be given to animals because cruelty to them, who do not count intrinsically, may encourage cruelty to humans, who do. "Common to . . . [all such] views is the proposition that we have no direct duties to animals; rather, animals are a sort of medium through which we may either succeed or fail to discharge those direct duties we owe to nonanimals, either ourselves, or other human beings, or, as in some views, God" (150).

This way of excluding animals from direct obligation, and yet somehow managing to give them some sort of moral standing, is now shown by Regan to be arbitrary rather than rationally grounded. Either the mistreatment of animals is wrong because it is inherently immoral, holds Regan, or such mistreatment has no necessary moral consequences for how we behave toward humans. There may be an emotional carryover from one to the other. A man who beats a dog is not likely to be a paragon of kindness to subordinates in his office. But the connection here is best explained as psychological rather than rational—it is a mental association, not a duty. Hence the idea of "indirect duty" to animals turns out to be fundamentally incoherent, and that dooms it as a solution to the problem of animals in moral theory. Duty to animals in the strict sense must follow from the basic principle directly. This leads one to suspect that there is something deeply wrong with the doctrine of the writers Regan discusses. We shall see later on that not only must Narveson be discarded, but also Kant and Rawls, at least in the present form of their positions. The failure of these thinkers to encompass animal rights directly betrays fundamental problems in their moral theories.

The ground is thus cleared for Regan to consider theories that hold that there is a clear duty of humans toward animals and that this duty is direct. Utilitarianism is the main example, and Regan rejects it for much the same reasons I have set out in chapter 1. But he puts special emphasis on the difficulty of interindividual comparisons of pleasure and pain. Absent a standard measure for comparison, Regan contends, Singer has no adequate basis for saying that all humans, let alone all animals, shall count as one when the aggregate of utility is added up.

I am not sure, however, that the problem of interpersonal comparisons in utilitarianism can be pushed to as deep a level as Regan's objection would have it. Your pleasure in music may be difficult to measure against mine, and when I assign a utility index number to each of us I know that I am making only a rough estimate. Yet it could still make sense to get an aggregate of utility by adding up the numbers. I could, of course, also do it in a more roundabout way. I could, say, count our pleasure in music as having the same place for each of us on each of our complex scales of marginal utility. Then, in adding up utilities to get an aggregate, I would incorporate differences between us by discounting your (or my) utilities by a certain percentage according to my estimate of our relative (and complex) efficiencies as hedonistic machines. The results would be the same by either procedure. Either way, this is but one great difficulty in utilitarianism; even were it set aside, the others are more than sufficient to rule it out as a moral principle.

The only other theory of duty that qualifies as direct, Regan now argues, is his own, which comes at the issue from a rights perspective. He begins by laying down a rule that he refers to as the harm principle. We have, he holds, *"a direct prima facie duty not to harm individuals."*[6] This rule, he argues, unquestionably applies to moral agents, and he calls it a principle rather than a reflective intuition or considered belief because it sums up or, better, unifies a number of intuitions that constrain us from doing harm to moral agents. That the rule is qualified as prima facie points to possible exceptions such as the use of force in self-defense. The basic rule seems to follow from the consideration that no one acting in any sort of moral universe whatever can inflict harm without alleging that there is some reason for it other than mere whim. The core meaning of the rule is later described as prohibiting the infliction of "gratuitous suffering."

The harm principle is then extended to cover animals. Regan has already shown that mammals of one year or more in age can suffer pain and frustration. He now appeals to a prereflective intuition that it is wrong on principle to inflict gratuitous suffering on them as well. He does not insist that a harm done to a moral patient is necessarily equal to the same harm inflicted on a moral agent. His point is only that we have a direct prima facie duty not to harm moral patients, without reference to any comparisons of the magnitude of wrong:

> The question at issue is not whether, say, killing a moral agent and a moral patient are, other things being equal, equally harmful. The question is whether we have any direct duties to moral patients. This question is logically distinct from the question about the *comparative magnitude* of harming a moral agent in a given way, on the one hand, and harming a moral patient in a similar way, on the other. For it may be true that harming either is directly wrong and yet the wrong when we do

some things to a moral agent (e.g. killing one) is a greater harm than
the harm done when we do the same to a moral patient.   (188)

Nevertheless, the harm principle still applies. As far as gratuitously
inflicted suffering is concerned, "all animals are equal." This is to
say, holds Regan, that all mammals of one year or more in age have
"inherent value," which, by its very nature, is the same for all.
Although animals cannot be moral agents because they cannot be
held responsible for following rules, they must be considered
"moral patients" because they can suffer unjustified harm from
moral agents. We thus come to a very essential, and often contested,
part of Regan's argument.

Having rejected utilitarianism, Regan is entitled to reject its view of
the individual as a mere receptacle for feelings of pleasure and pain,
which can then be aggregated. The rights alternative is rather to treat
the very subjectivity of the individual entity as inherently valuable in
itself. It is valued not because it has fared, or will fare, well or ill, but
simply for its own sake, because it has a life that is "its own." Regan
begins by expounding this principle as it applies to moral agents:

> The inherent value of individual moral agents is to be understood as
> being conceptually distinct from the intrinsic value that attaches to
> the experiences they have (e.g. their pleasures or preference satisfac-
> tions), as not being reducible to values of the latter kind, and as being
> incommensurate with these values. . . . The inherent value of any given
> moral agent isn't equal to the sum of intrinsic values, neither the
> intrinsic value of that individual's experiences nor the total of the
> intrinsic value of the experiences of all other moral agents [and
> patients].
>
> *Individual moral agents themselves have a distinctive kind of value*,
> according to the postulate of inherent value, but not according to the
> receptacle view to which utilitarians are committed. It's the cup, not
> just what goes into it, that is valuable.   (235–236)

Animals too, according to the harm principle, are not mere receptacles of units of utility. With this thought, the way is now prepared

for the crucial move in Regan's argument. Inherent value, by its very nature and definition, is independent of the pleasures and pains that the subject has or will feel. It lies merely in the fact of subjectivity, in being that which can and does have feelings. Hence inherent value is equal and the same in all who have it; this means that it is the same in moral patients as it is in moral agents:

> If we postulate inherent value in the case of moral agents and recognize the need to view *their* possession of it as being equal, then we will be rationally obliged to do the same in the case of moral patients. *All* who have inherent value thus have it equally, whether they be moral agents or moral patients. . . . Inherent value is thus a *categorical* concept. One either has it, or one does not. There are no in-betweens. Moreover, all those who have it, have it equally. It does not come in degrees. (240–41)

Another way of putting this principle, I suggest, is to reflect that the life of every sentient being is as important to that individual as our life is to us. It is not a question of anything like "better" or "richer." The life of a dog, of an ant, or of a human is the only life it will ever have. It is inevitably finite, and once it is over it is infinitely gone. In that sense all sentient lives have an inherent equal value.

This principle of equal inherent value thus confirms Regan's earlier application of the rule of formal justice to the harm principle:

> When these common harms are at issue, to affirm that we have a direct duty to moral agents not to harm them but deny this in the case of moral patients is to flout the requirement of formal justice or impartiality, requiring, as it does, that similar cases be treated dissimilarly. And that is to fall far short of making an ideal moral judgment. (189)

Regan thus adopts an egalitarian view of formal justice in which the mere subjectivity of individuals requires that they be treated equally. But formal justice means treating *equals* equally, and it is therefore subject to another problem. It is at least logically consistent with "perfectionism," or the kind of hierarchy of values of the sort we find in Aristotle. On this basis the principle of formal justice does not necessarily lead to equal treatment. One individual might be justly subordinated to another.

Regan, however, justifiably rules out perfectionism, no less than utilitarianism, albeit from a different angle. It too is counterintuitive because it violates so many of our considered beliefs that it must be discarded as a unifying principle of morals. But with both utilitarianism and perfectionism eliminated, all that is left is to treat all animals as having equal value.

In this context Regan does not pause to consider a possible objection based on Kant. One could say that rationality alone is valuable, so that the harm principle applies only to rational beings. But Regan has already given an implicit answer to this by showing that the idea of an indirect duty to animals is not sustainable. Kant's restriction of equality to humans presupposes that animals are things. But there is a difference between a rock and a dog that philosophy cannot simply pass over.

A follower of Albert Schweitzer, on the other hand, might protest that the scope of inherent value in Regan is too narrow. It ought to be extended to include all that is included in Schweitzer's "reverence for life." Regan, however, is justifiably reluctant to be that inclusive. He acknowledges that his idea of inherent value has much in common with Schweitzer's reverence for life, which he feels is potentially too broad:

> It is not clear why we have, or how we could be reasonable be said to have, direct duties to, say, individual blades of grass, potatoes, or cancer cells. Yet all are alive, and so all should be owed direct duties if all have inherent value. Nor is it clear why we have, or how we reasonably could be said to have, direct duties to collections of such individuals— to lawns, potato fields, or cancerous tumors. (242)

Merely being alive therefore seems not to be enough for inherent value to be ascribed. Regan, however, wisely refrains from entering into controversy as to how broadly the notion of inherent value may be extended.

Regan is now ready for a final step linking this whole set of reasonings. He brings forward what he calls the "respect principle," which states that individuals having equal inherent value are entitled to treatment respectful of that value:

> If individuals have equal inherent value, then any principle that declares what treatment is due them as a matter of justice must take their equal value into account. The following principle (*the respect principle*) does this: *We are to treat those individuals who have inherent value in ways that respect their inherent value.* Now, the respect principle sets forth an egalitarian, nonperfectionist interpretation of formal justice. . . . It enjoins us to treat *all* those individuals having inherent value in ways that respect their value, and thus it requires respectful treatment of those who satisfy the subject-of-a-life criterion. (248)

Regan's main conclusion at this point is that individuals may not be harmed, as in utilitarianism, in order to bring about the best aggregate consequences. "To borrow part of a phrase from Kant, individuals who have inherent value must never be treated *merely as a means* to securing the best aggregate consequences" (249). His discussion of the respect principle then ends with the thought that it requires assistance to animals as well as respect.

Thus far, the only objection I have raised concerning Regan's argument has to do with his criterion as to what range of animals is entitled to moral consideration. As Francione has argued, there is no reason why every animal that can feel pain and experience pleasure does not have as much prima facie right as any other according to the harm principle, and the same prima facie claim to inherent value and respect.[7] We do wrong, I believe, if we go out of our way to crush an innocuous beetle that happens to cross our path. Indeed, if that beetle were drowning in a pool of water near us, and we were able to reach it with a branch or pole, we would do wrong not to give it assistance.

Regan himself says that the line between those individuals who are subjects of a life and those who are not is hard to draw, and that in any case he considers the subject-of-a-life criterion as a sufficient but not a necessary condition for inclusion in the protective scope of the harm principle:

> Second, and relatedly, the argument of the present section does not logically preclude the possibility that those humans and animals who fail to meet the subject-of-a-life criterion nonetheless have inherent value. Since the claim is made only that meeting this criterion is a sufficient condition of making the attribution of inherent value intelligible and nonarbitrary, it remains possible that animals that are conscious but not capable of acting intentionally, or, say, permanently comatose human beings might nonetheless be viewed as having inherent value.[8]

This limitation in Regan, if indeed it is such, is minor and can be resolved in different ways. The basic argument from inherent value, however, depends on a somewhat shadowy initial assumption which requires more discussion. Before turning to that, a brief summation of Regan's argument in outline might be helpful:

1. He rejects utilitarianism and perfectionism as counterintuitive, and he dismisses Kant and Rawls because the indirect duty concept of regard for animals is a failure.

2. The rule of formal justice, that individuals must be treated equally insofar as they are similar, is the consequence of rejecting utilitarianism. The rule of equal formal justice, that individuals have an equal right not to be harmed, is the consequence of rejecting perfectionism.

3. That all human individuals have inherent value follows from the rejection of the utilitarian view that the value of individuals is measured by their feelings of pain or pleasure.

4. Having rejected any version of indirect duty, and on the quite reasonable assumption that we owe at least "some" duty to all mammals of a year or more in age, we must conclude that these latter have inherent value also.

5. An individual either has inherent value or does not. There is no middle ground. Hence all mammals are equal in inherent value.

6. Recognition of inherent value requires us to respect it. This respect principle is now shown to underlie the harm principle which prima facie forbids harming any individual.

This structure of reasoning, solid in itself, depends on the initial observation that "[n]o serious moral thinker accepts the view that animals may be treated in just any way we please" (150). It is this observation that leads into his rejection of the idea of indirect duty and thence to the rest of his entire case. It seems to me, however, that the initial statement has to be more than an empirical generalization as to what serious thinkers say. It has to be a categorical requirement, and indeed Regan may well think of it that way despite the modesty of his language. Nevertheless, the point must be made and must be justified. Otherwise, a critic could conjure up a theorist who claims not to care one whit for the suffering of animals, human infants, or human mental defectives. He or she could claim to be interested solely in Regan's "moral agents." Indeed, a hardhearted Rawlsian could also say that. Such a writer might admit a soft spot for animals, and even recognize that a goodly number of other humans also feel that way, and still consistently maintain that humans owe them nothing.

I do not believe, of course, that decent and responsible moral theorists would make that theoretical argument a recommendation for moral practice by their readers. But they might make the point as a strictly abstract objection. The critics may want to arrive at the same result as Regan's and yet feel obliged to protest that the route he has taken will not get there.

A truly fundamental ground for Regan's case is therefore lacking. I think, however, that such a ground can be supplied. The problem in Regan's argument seems to arise from dismissing Kant too quickly. Kant's exclusion of animals from direct moral standing on an equal basis with humans can be shown to be a major error in his moral theory. The range of beings to which the categorical imperative applies cannot be limited to humans and other rational beings. Unless it is to fall into inner inconsistency it must also apply to animals, human infants, and mental defectives as well. The result, I shall try to show in chapter 3, is that the second form of Kant's categorical imperative must be reworded as follows: *Treat sentience in yourself as well as others never as a means only, but at the same time also as an end.*

Before turning to that argument, however, I think it best to dispose of two other objections to Regan's case which I think are insubstantial.

In his book *The Animals Issue* (1992), Peter Carruthers puts forward two main objections to Regan's claim that animals have rights. The first has to do with what he describes as Regan's intuitionism. Regan, he insists, is basically an intuitionist in his view of animal rights, even though he does not make much use of the term, speaking instead of "reflective equilibrium."[9] Carruthers objects that any argument from moral intuitionism is "unacceptable." He offers a number of reasons arranged in sequence as if in a legal brief (17–20):

1. The moral values we supposedly intuit in objects do not exist in the natural world.

2. They do not explain the behavior of the beings to which they are applied.

3. They do not explain differences in assigning degrees of value (as for example between animals and humans).

4. If moral values do not exist in nature, how can they affect our minds?

5. Even if moral values could affect our minds, what survival advantage would explain their selection in the course of the evolution of the human species? Our intuition of moral values in an object might at least be unreliable.

6. Not everybody's intuition would be the same.

I do not believe that these objections, as applied to Regan, are sustainable:

1. No one has claimed that moral values must exist naturally in Carruthers's sense. The value in a piece of gold is in our valuation of it. The value of an animal, friend, or spouse lies in objective quali-

ties that we value. In the case of animals (even apart from pets, etc.) the cause of valuing is our empathy with the pain or joy they feel.

2. No one ever supposed that value explains the behavior of the object valued. Diamonds are valuable because they sparkle; they do not sparkle because they are valuable.

3. Regan, at least, does not attribute prima facie differences of value to the sentient beings with which his theory is concerned. There may be relevant differences of value where a conflict of otherwise legitimate interests occurs between the beings he has in mind. But apart from that very carefully delimited exception, all the human and nonhuman animals covered have "equal inherent value." This is a point Regan frequently repeats.

4. The moral values don't affect our minds; the pains or joys of animals external to us do.

5. Since moral valuation is not directly a cognitive issue, there is no reason why it should not be reliable. We usually make some reasonable estimate as to whether an animal is suffering pain or enjoying pleasure. The evolutionary advantage of such sensibility is clear.

6. There is a great difference between immediate intuitive response, which is what Carruthers takes to be the issue, and reflective intuition. The first is prereflective and can vary widely in different individuals. The second is not an immediate response to an individual or individual situation. It is the outcome of careful reflection on a principle which prereflective intuition recommends. The solidity of Regan's reasoning, once the initial ground is supplied, is clear from the summation laid out above.

Carruthers's second objection to the rights approach is that it is not really a proper theory since it does not explain morality or tell us why we should be moral:

> [W]e need to be told what it is about morality that enables it to claim such a central place in our lives. . . .
>
> We can say . . . that there are two main requirements that a moral theory must meet, if it is to be rationally acceptable. The first is that its governing conception must give a plausible picture of the source of

morality, and of the origins of moral motivation. This is where Regan fails altogether. The second is less deeply theoretical, but equally important. It is that the basic normative principle or principles of the theory should yield intuitively acceptable consequences. . . . It is simply that a good moral theory must entail at least a fair proportion of our considered moral beliefs, at the cost, otherwise, of becoming unbelievable. Any moral theory that could justify arbitrary killings of innocents, for example, is going to be unacceptable, no matter how satisfying it may seem in respect of its governing conception. . . . [My] next chapter will be occupied with exploring the relative strengths and weaknesses of utilitarianism and contractualism along each of these two dimensions. (24)

The first part of this two-pronged objection has some merit. In the last analysis, Regan does not supply what could be called a truly "governing conception of morality," and I shall attempt to show in the next chapter how that lack can be supplied. Nevertheless, Regan's respect principle and its implications for the treatment of inherent value are largely satisfactory even as they stand. It is simply wrong to do what root intuition, which can be sustained on due reflection, tells us it is wrong to do! Carruthers is mistaken in his understanding of what Regan means by the role of intuition in moral life, and so he is also mistaken in his belief that Regan "fails altogether" in his treatment of morality.

Evelyn B. Pluhar, in *Beyond Prejudice: The Moral Significance of Human and Nonhuman Animals* is also critical of Regan's appeal to intuition, and I believe that she too has not completely credited his distinction between an intuition as a prereflective gut reaction and as a reflectively justified principle. That is not her most important criticism, however. She is much more concerned with the apparent movement of Regan's argument from our human concern for fellow humans who are mentally deficient to concern for animal subjects-of-a-life on the grounds that both are indistinguishable as "moral patients."[10] Thus, if we are bound to refrain from killing infants we don't particularly want or mental defectives who are a burden, we must also be restrained from killing unwanted animals since they too are moral patients.[11] Their reactions to pain and their level of intelligent awareness are no less than those of infants and defectives, and are sometimes even greater.

This argument is generally known in the literature on animal welfare as the "Argument from Marginal Cases,"[12] and Pluhar dissects it with relentless elaboration and acute insight. She begins by showing that the argument from marginal cases cannot be deflated by denying the transition from human to animal moral patients. One deflationary strategy is to invoke the slippery slope. Animals and marginal humans can indeed be compared, this argument concedes, but in principle neither is entitled to moral standing. The only reason to grant moral standing to human moral patients is the fear that we will not be able to draw the line between the normal and the subnormal. Once we were free in principle to exploit submarginal humans, there would be no stopping point. Humans who are simply dull rather than submarginal would be at risk. Hence we grant moral standing to all humans, marginal or not, but deny it to animals.

Much the same kind of argument can be derived from what might be called benevolent speciesism—the idea, which can take a variety of forms, that living individuals having the shape of a human being are entitled to the respect we generally owe to our species. Otherwise, we would again face the allegedly insoluble problem of drawing the line of marginality.

In reply to all such arguments Pluhar notes that many societies have practiced infanticide and/or the euthanasia of the old or deformed without consequence for social stability in other respects. She also points out that many people do not object but rather agree with the idea of getting rid of a deformed child or adult as a useless and offensive burden. Thus far Pluhar's findings are favorable to Regan. If one starts from the premise that the test of morality is the treatment of the *normal* human being, then one cannot avoid a dreadful consequence. Submarginal human beings could be treated as callously as animals:

> No morally relevant difference between marginal humans and sentient nonhumans has been found to legitimize the very different ways

in which these beings are standardly treated. . . . One must either give up the belief that autonomous moral agents are the *primary* subjects of moral concern and respect, or one must accept the full, ghastly (for marginal humans and sentient nonhumans alike) implications of that view.[13]

But this is not the end of it for Pluhar. Regan's case for animal rights ultimately depends on his respect principle—on the principle that all subjects-of-a-life must be given equal consideration. Most rationalists, however, would find this equation unacceptable. The test of moral considerability for them is almost always rational capacity. Neither animals nor marginal humans have that capacity. Hence, argues Pluhar, by the criterion of rationality, neither group qualifies as objects of our moral obligations (239).

Which moral theory, asks Pluhar, shall we then accept? That Regan's position passes all the tests which he lays down for moral principles is not perhaps to be denied. One must treat submarginal humans and animals in the same way—with respect. But how are competing norms, which also pass his test, to be excluded? What is ultimately wrong with saying that the interests of *both* submarginal humans and animals can be ignored? This, then, is how Pluhar formulates what she takes to be Regan's dilemma:

He is absolutely correct in pointing out that arguments are wanting that give primacy to moral agency, to higher degrees of intelligence-related capacities, to the agent's self-interest, or to units of non-moral good as opposed to individuals. Followers of such views would counter, of course, that his rights view is no less arbitrary. Once one's reflective intuitions agree with Regan's claim that we owe direct duties to humans who are not moral agents, the rest falls into place: we cannot accept this contention and consistently deny that relevantly similar nonhumans are owed no direct duties. But that initial agreement need never occur—unless we can find an argument to support it. (239–240)

Pluhar believes that Regan not only has not, but cannot, find such an argument. She thinks, however, that she has found a purely rationalist argument which can provide a sure foundation for the conclusion Regan wants to reach. I shall take up that position in chapter 4.

The issue Pluhar raises is important, and her analysis of it is impeccable. But I do not agree that the argument from marginal cases is as decisive for Regan's position as she thinks. He used that argument in his *All That Dwell Therein* (1982), and he repeats it in all of his subsequent arguments for animal rights. It is especially prominent in his criticisms of Kant, who is most obviously exposed to the *concursus horribilium* which follows from treating any subrational entity as a thing. This is the context in which he endorses the marginal cases argument in *Defending Animal Rights*, which appeared in 2001.[14] But at no point does Regan make this the crux of his theory. He starts from the prereflective intuition that animals cannot be treated in just any way at all and then moves on to the idea of inherent value and the respect principle. I do agree with Pluhar, though, that this starting position is not yet adequately justified.

Finally, I should like to conclude this chapter with a brief comment on the one extended argument for animal rights that runs more or less in parallel with Regan's. Francione arrives at conclusions much like Regan's, though starting from a different point of view. Francione is a jurist and proceeds from a critique of the fateful ambiguity, in law as well as common speech, as to what is humane and permissible in the treatment of animals. The infliction of "unnecessary" suffering is considered wrong by most people and is often prohibited by law. But in public opinion and in jurisprudence, animals are taken to be property, and Francione argues that so long as animals continue to be regarded by the law as property all the rules against "unnecessary" pain will be construed by the courts in favor of the property owner and against the interest of the animals.[15] They will always be treated as "research animals," "food animals," etc. If this somewhat overstates the case, it nonetheless correctly states the tendency. In Francione's effective way of putting it, animals are not taken by the law to be sensitive entities whose deepest interest, no different from our own, is to avoid suffering. They are always regarded as means to human ends.

I believe that Regan's argument from inherent value is more fundamental and complete than Francione's. But *Introduction to Animal Rights* is a persuasive appeal to the principle of equal consideration and is thus a valuable addition to the literature of animal rights.

Regan's argument has therefore not been refuted or replaced. The only open question, then, on the rights approach to animal interests remains as it has been put above. How can Regan's solid and imposing superstructure be more fundamentally grounded? I shall try to answer that question in the next chapter.

3

Animal Rights and Kant

Kant most emphatically did not believe that respect for animals is a necessary consequence of the categorical imperative. Animals are not autonomous or self-conscious in Kant's sense, and so cannot be considered moral agents. For Kant, moral obligations and moral rights apply to agents alone. As moral patients, animals are accorded no respect. They are simply lumped together with mere things as far as the theory of moral standing is concerned.

Nevertheless, the meaning of the categorical imperative and thus of the moral law, as presented in the *Groundwork*, has been misinterpreted not only by the commentators but by Kant himself. It cannot be construed as denying animals the status of moral patients, for if that is done, Kant's moral theory collapses into incoherence. This is not to deny that the categorical imperative is a firm foundation for rational morality. Properly interpreted, Kant's idea of moral law turns out, surprisingly enough, to be the most powerful of all arguments for the rights of all sentient beings. In what follows I shall attempt to show the force of these contentions. I propose to take up the main forms of the categorical imperative in order to demonstrate that they are incoherent as they stand, and that this incoherence can be remedied only by including all sentient beings as moral patients.

The Formula of Universal Law (FUL)

One way of deriving a particular categorical imperative is to universalize some maxim of policy that a moral agent proposes to adopt. This is the first form of the categorical imperative. The difficulty that underlies it as it is characteristically interpreted can be seen as soon as we reflect on the scope of the legitimate and relevant maxims to be tested by this method.

A legitimate maxim, for Kant, has to be one that can be properly universalized. One cannot, in stating a maxim, put arbitrary limitations on its scope. To say "I shall lie whenever it suits my interest" is a perfect example of a maxim that can be properly tested; it leads to the conclusion that, if that maxim were universalized and everybody practiced it as a policy, its very point would be destroyed. Everyone would tell lies, and no one would believe them. Hence a rule against lying follows logically.

Not all policies having the form of a maxim can be properly generalized. One cannot qualify the maxim to suit one's special situation. I cannot say, for example, that I may lie whenever it advantages my family (named), profession (described), or ethnic group (identified). This statement of policy could obviously withstand universalization. It would not produce the kind of contradiction or absurdity that indicates a categorical imperative: one must not lie.[1] But it would have no universal or morally fundamental meaning.

Commenting on the formula of humanity (FH) as an end in itself, Thomas Pogge makes this point incisively. "The sharpening of the categorical imperative through Formula II [FH] is important," says Pogge,

> in yet another context, namely for the assessment of maxims that contain a reference to a subset of all persons, e.g. to women, parents, Muslims, Canadians, or the poor. When the question is merely what

the agent can will by way of maxims available to all persons, then some outrageous maxims might seem to pass.[2]

A striking example of such an illicit maxim is given by Pogge in an extended note: "As Europeans we can reasonably will that all Europeans may colonize" (211).

I would hold that this way of misusing FUL applies to the status of animals as well. Maxims that exclude respect for animals—for example, I will eat the meat of any kind of animal that suits my taste—seem at first thought to be universalizable. The maxim's adoption by everyone does not threaten my freedom to pursue my policy or my possible success in doing so. I can eat as much meat as I please, while others are free to do so or not to do so as they wish. But this result follows only because the above maxim is implicitly restricted to nonhumans. The meat that we may eat at our pleasure, in other words, is tacitly assumed to be the flesh of animals. On the basis of that assumption, the maxim can be universalized without absurdity. But once the silent restriction to animals is recognized and removed, the carnivore is swept into the maxim's compass. It now says that I will eat the flesh of any sentient being as I please, so the result of universalization is now quite problematic. The policy, universalized, leads to the possibility and legitimacy of cannibalism. There would now be a universal law permitting me to eat all others, but allowing all others, including humans, to eat me.

The same considerations also apply to Thomas Pogge's variant formulation of FUL, which is based on an "atypical" construction of the principle. According to the standard view of FUL, the maxim of a will, when universalized, is to be evaluated as if it were a rule that everybody *will* follow. According to Pogge's reconstruction, the universalization of a maxim should be taken only as permissive. It merely makes that maxim *available* to everybody, who *may* then use it if they want to:

> Strictly speaking, it is then not his maxim that the agent must be able to will as a universal law, but the *availability* of this maxim. Other things being unchanged, can he will our world to be such that every-

one feels (morally) free to—and those so inclined ("by nature") actually do—adopt his maxim? This differs from what the categorical
imperative is usually taken to demand, namely that the agent must be
able to will that everyone *actually* adopt his maxim.   (190)

With this revised interpretation, Pogge writes, the formula of universal law will screen out maxims, not on the grounds that they
would lead to contradiction (the traditional interpretation) but
because making them available to real people under given or
expected empirical conditions would render them useless. The best
example of what he has in mind is the maxim that, if I am in need, I
may borrow money deceitfully to ease my condition:

> In the world to be imagined, everyone would be free to adopt the
> maxim "when in need, to make deceitful promises so as to alleviate my
> difficulties." Thus people in need would (be known to) have no reason
> not to make deceitful promises; potential promisees would (be known
> to) have good reason to reject promises made by persons in need; and
> most people in evident need thus might not even bother to offer
> promises—deceitfully or otherwise. But this shows at most that if the
> maxim were universally permitted, it would fall into disuse as it were.
> It does not show that the world we are imagining is impossible.   (191)

It might thus be argued, against what we have said above, that permission to eat meat, even if it applied in principle to humans, would
not be used that way. People just aren't cannibals, or at least they do
not hunger for the flesh of fellow humans very often. Permission to
eat human flesh would thus be available but hardly used. This perhaps is why Kant's exclusion of animals does not seem a critical issue
to Pogge.[3]

But this restatement of Kant's principle does not achieve its goal.
The universal rule, in many cases, would not lead to universal disuse.
Some needy persons, for example, might be able to hide the usual
signs of their condition and so be able to borrow deceitfully. The rule
against lying would not then fall into general disuse. It would still be
useful to some and would not be discarded universally. Even worse

for Pogge's interpretation is the maxim "I will murder my rivals or opponents whenever I can do so safely and effectively." Mere availability of that policy universally would not destroy society. Most people dislike killing "by nature." In any event, only very bold and aggressive types would take the risk of being caught by the police. Hence the outcome of Pogge's version would be at odds with that of the standard interpretation. An antisocial maxim such as the one on murder would not be fully ruled out by the formula of universal law.

Pogge's variation, furthermore, would also seem to be ruled out by anticipating the second form of the categorical imperative which states that humans may not be treated merely as means. If I am successful in getting a loan that I do not intend to pay back by hiding my poverty, or if I am successful in murdering a rival by acting with great secrecy and prudence, I am using some other person as a means to my own advantage and thus violate my obligation not to treat humanity only as a means but also at the same time as an end.[4]

The basic rule of FUL thus does not admit exceptions and does not escape the difficulty we have raised. If we reformulate the maxim about eating meat to make it truly universal in its scope—that is, if we apply it to humans as well as animals—we come to recognize a basic right in animals. The relevant imperative now is that sentient creatures must not be eaten. Extending the idea in more or less obvious ways, we can conclude that the moral universe of the first and central form of the categorical imperative includes sentient as well as rational beings. This does not mean, of course, that nonhuman animals are no less bound than humans to be vegetarians. Rational beings alone are moral agents, and they alone are subjects of the moral law, which is imposed on them alone by the force of reason. But animals are now included as moral patients in the universe to which the law must apply.

Suppose, then, as Pogge suggests, that FUL is read in the light of FH, the idea of humanity as an end in itself. Would our extension of the scope of FUL to animals still be justified? We shall try to show later on that, in this second form as well, the scope is unacceptably narrow, and that the reference to humanity must be replaced by sentience. The categorical imperative, thus revised, would read: Act in such a way that you always treat sentience, whether in your self or the self of any other sentient being, never simply as a means but at the same time as an end.[5]

This result is obviously at odds with Kant's flat denial that animals have moral standing, for he refers to them not only as "things" but as "instruments" for human use.[6] Kant sometimes speaks of teleology as an aid to understanding nature. One philosophical position he could have used to justify his view of animals as instruments would have been some sort of natural teleology à la Aristotle. But Aristotle's teleology was out of fashion at the time and was surely unacceptable to Kant. For him teleology was but a heuristic device, not a metaphysical or scientific principle:

> Thus when, for example, we say that the crystalline lens in the eye has the *purpose* of accomplishing by a second refraction of the light rays the focusing of those emanating from a point on the retina, all that is said is that the representation of a purpose in nature's causal action in creating an eye is to be thought because such an idea functions as a principle for conducting research concerning the lens of the eye, and likewise to help find the means which one might devise to expedite the result. In so doing there is not attributed to nature a causality by the representation of ends—i.e. *intentional* action—which would be a determining teleological judgement, and as such a transcendent one since it instances a causality lying beyond the bounds of nature.[7]

Teleology, therefore, cannot be invoked to justify the denial of moral status to animals. In light of what was said about the first form of the categorical imperative, we have a direct obligation to acknowledge that animals have rights. We cannot, therefore, go along with Kant in attempting to circumvent the issue of true rights in animals by talk of duties that are "indirect." For "indirect" duties to animals, as Kant and others understand it, is not a duty to them at all. It is merely an indirect duty to other humans:

> But so far as animals are concerned we have no direct duties. Animals are not self-conscious and are there merely as a means to an end.

That end is man. We can ask, "Why do animals exist?" But to ask, "Why does man exist?" is a meaningless question. Our duties toward animals are merely indirect duties towards humanity. Thus, if a dog has served his master long and faithfully, his service, on the analogy of human service, deserves reward and when the dog has grown too old to serve, his master ought to keep him until he dies. Such action helps to support us in our duties towards human beings, where they are bounden duties. If then any acts of animals are analogous to human acts and spring from the same principles, we have duties toward the animals because thus we cultivate the corresponding duties toward human beings. If a man shoots his dog because the animal is no longer capable of service, he does not fail in his duty to the dog, for the dog cannot judge, but his act is inhuman and damages in himself that humanity which it is his duty to show towards mankind. If he is not to stifle his human feelings, he must practice kindness towards animals, for he who is cruel to animals becomes hard also in his dealings with men.[8]

This idea of indirect duty is an old one. It is clearly stated in St. Thomas,[9] and goes back at least to the Greeks.[10] But I have already noted that it has been criticized effectively, and I might add a few more comments to show that it cannot be sustained. If the infliction of pain and death on animals, without legitimating cause, is not cruel per se, why should it harden us toward humans? And if it does in fact harden us toward humans, it must be because we have become insensitive to the *wrongful* harming of animals. As Broadie and Pybus put it,

Whatever is not an end in itself cannot be an object of direct moral concern. But Kant holds that animals are not ends in themselves. If, therefore, we are to speak, as Kant wishes, of maltreating an animal, we are to speak of something which is not an object of direct moral concern. Now maltreatment is a moral concept, in so far as it refers to a mode of dealing with objects which is unfitting to their nature. But if animals are not objects of direct moral concern, then in what can maltreatment of them consist?[11]

Hence the idea of indirect duty is no more able than teleology to mitigate the weakness of the categorical imperative with respect to animals. But since the idea of indirect duty to animals is so pervasive in the literature and such a common way of soothing troubled consciences, it may be appropriate to quote Robert Nozick's eloquent and devastating critique:

> Some say people should not do so [kill animals wantonly] because such acts brutalize them and make them more likely to take the lives of *persons*, solely for pleasure. These acts that are morally unobjectionable in themselves, they say, have an undesirable moral spillover. (Things then would be different if there were no possibility of such a spillover—for example, for the person who knows himself to be the last person on earth.) But why *should* there be such a spillover? If it is, in itself, perfectly all right to do anything at all to animals for any reason whatsoever, then provided a person realizes the clear line between animals and persons and keeps it in mind as he acts, why should killing animals tend to brutalize him and make him more likely to harm or kill persons? Do butchers commit more murders? (Than other persons who have knives around?) If I enjoy hitting a baseball squarely with a bat, does this significantly increase the danger of my doing the same to someone's head? Am I not capable of understanding that people differ from baseballs, and doesn't this understanding stop the spillover? Why should things be different in the case of animals? To be sure, it is an empirical question whether spillover does take place or not; but there *is* a puzzle as to why it should, at least among readers of this essay, sophisticated people who are capable of drawing distinctions and differentially acting upon them.[12]

The exclusion of animals from direct moral consideration cannot be justified by any argument of the sort used by Kant. There is thus no alternative to acknowledging a fundamental weakness in Kant's initial formulation of the moral law. FUL lays a moral obligation on moral agents only. Yet the wording of the rule illicitly expands its scope to cover rights as well. The first form of the categorical imperative, i.e.,

FUL, strongly suggests and was clearly meant to imply that duties exist only toward other humans, who alone have moral standing. This turns out to be misleading, and yet there is nothing that can be added to the first form of the categorical imperative that would easily clarify the scope of the moral universe to which we now see it ought to apply. We simply have to be aware that it is phrased in terms of obligations only. If the scope of *rights* appears to be confined to rational beings, it is only because of Kant's (and perhaps our) implicit speciesism.

The Formula of Humanity as an End in Itself

If Kant's limitation on the scope of rights is to be saved, it will have to follow from the *independent* validity of the second form of the categorical imperative (FH). The wording in Kant's formulation is as follows:

> Act in such a way that you always treat humanity whether in your own person or the person of any other, never simply as a means, but always at the same time as an end.[13]

There is, as we shall see, some uncertainty among the commentators as to the scope of this principle. But as far as I can see, it is merely another way of stating the formula of universal law. FUL states the categorical imperative in terms of the legitimacy of maxims; FH states it in terms of the legitimacy of ends or goals.

In FH, Kant is referring to "subjective" grounds of the will's determination, which is what he means by "an *end*." His first form of the categorical imperative deals only with the *formal principles of the will*, which are abstracted from all ends whatever. The second form deals with the *ends of the will*, that is, with its subjective goals. These ends or goals are most often the results of impulses arising from material needs that are only "relative" to passing inclinations. "They can provide no universal principles." But the "goal" of humanity, says Kant, is radically different from a relative end. It is an "objective" end, of "absolute value" and thus an "end in itself":

Suppose, however, there were something *whose existence* has *in itself* absolute value, something which as *an end in itself* could be a ground of determinate laws; then in it, and in it alone, would there be a ground of a possible categorical imperative—that is, of a practical law.

Now I say that man, and in general every rational being, *exists* as an end in himself, *not merely as a means* for arbitrary use by this or that will. (95 [428])

In this statement, the phrase "whose existence in itself has absolute value" is far less powerful than might appear. It refers merely to something which must *never* be taken as a means but *always* treated as an end. Read thus, there is no good reason, in this statement of FH or in Kant's illustrations of the principle, to explain why animals should not also be included. On this point, indeed, Kant falls into simple dogmatism:

The value of all objects that can *be produced* by our action is always conditioned [on our inclinations]. Beings whose existence depends, not on our will, but on nature, have none the less, if they are non-rational beings only a relative value as means and are consequently called *things*. Rational beings, on the other hand, are called *persons*, because their nature already marks them out as ends in themselves— that is, as something not to be used merely as a means—and consequently imposes to that extent a limit on all arbitrary treatment of them (and is an object of reverence). (96, [428])

Kant provides four illustrations as to how FH can be applied. In the first illustration, he rules out suicide as a way to "escape from a painful situation." This act would mean construing one's person only as a means to a tolerable existence. Kant could just as well have made his point in terms of "sentient existence" or just "sentience." Sentient existence implies hope in the future, and to give that up is to use one's "person" as a means. The root of FH is an appeal to our basic intuition that the most precious thing in our existence should not be sacrificed for anything less. But nothing is more precious than hope; and even a fly, desperately buzzing to get through a window, must have hope of some sort if it is conscious at all.

In Kant's second illustration, making a false promise to another is using that person as a mere means, and therefore it too is forbidden. This is not to say that another person can never be used as a means. The very fact of social interaction makes that inevitable. But on the principle of FH the person used must participate in the end. One must not "make use of another man *merely as a means* to an end he does not share" (97 [429]). Domesticated animals, however, can surely share in the end for which they are used if they are adequately compensated for their efforts. In this respect they differ from human workers in that their participation is involuntary. But workers may share in the benefits of the end without necessarily endorsing it, as long as the compensation is adequate. Hence animals should not be used merely as means and kept or discarded as mere thinglike instruments. The dog retired for old age and the horse put out to pasture after long service are not beneficiaries of mere kindness as Kant would have it; but rather they are entitled to share in the benefits they helped to produce.

In the third illustration, Kant requires us to develop our "capacities for greater perfection." Neglect of these capacities may be "compatible with the *maintenance* of humanity as an end in itself, but not with the *promotion* of this end" (98 [430]). It is not immediately clear what Kant means by "greater perfection." He can hardly mean it literally since perfection is absolute; it has no degrees of more or less.[14] It is more likely that he is thinking of skills, such as the ability to play chess, solve mathematical problems, and so on. But these are means only to material goals and are therefore only "relative." It may be, of course, that the discipline acquired in playing chess, solving mathematical problems, or mopping floors efficiently may help us overcome inclinations that bar the way to moral rationality. But any such connection would be indirect or accidental, and Kant does not have that in mind.

The meaning of illustration three becomes clear once we read it in the light of the fourth and final illustration. The subject now is "happiness" considered to be "the natural end which all men seek." Kant comments that it is not enough simply to refrain from interfering with humanity's *pursuit* of happiness:

> This is . . . merely negatively and not positively to agree with *humanity as an end in itself* unless every one endeavours also, so far as in him lies, to further the ends of others, for the ends of a subject who is an end in himself must, if this conception is to have its *full* effect in me, be also, as far as possible, my ends. (98 [430])

In this illustration of FH, the ends considered are clearly empirical and relative ends. If others, for example, are in need of shelter, I must help to build a house. Thus all of humanity's happiness taken as my end would only be an aggregate of the empirical ends of all individuals. But with this understanding of promoting happiness FH ought to be extended to include not only humans but all sentient beings. If it is intuitively wrong not to help another human being in trouble where that is feasible, then it is also wrong not to help an animal where that is feasible. We may not be strictly obliged to get food to a hungry elk somewhere in the forest. But we may be strictly obliged to rescue a bug that is drowning in a puddle at our feet.

We may now go back to the third illustration of FH. Its point, it is now clear, is that we are obliged to perfect the skills that may make us more useful to other humans. In the light of what we have just said about the fourth illustration, however, we are also obliged to develop skills that may be helpful to other sentients as well.

The second form of the categorical imperative must accordingly be rephrased as FS rather than FH: *Act in such a way that you always treat sentience in your own existence or in the existence of any other, never simply as a means, but also as an end.*

It follows, therefore, that the second formulation of the categorical imperative cannot be interpreted as a determination of the scope of the first. Thus Thomas Pogge, conceding that the scope of FUL, if taken alone, might give protection to nonrational beings, considers this possibility to have been ruled out by Kant's language in FH, which expressly refers to humans only:

The fact that all and only rational beings can apply, and are bound by, the universalization requirement [in FUL] does not entail that all and only rational beings are protected by it. Formulas I [FUL] and Ia [the law of nature], though providing the *form* of the supreme principle of morality, offer no suggestion for how the *scope* of the required universalization is to be determined.

My alternative interpretation views Formula II [FH] as contributing precisely this determination, in two steps:

B1. As rational beings, we recognize as ends in themselves exactly those beings who have a telos that is of absolute value. However, only a good will has absolute value. Therefore, exactly those beings who have the potential for a good will qualify for the status of ends in themselves.

This argument provides what Kant needs: a way of showing just whom moral reasoning must take into account, and on what grounds. The argument singles out human beings—or rather persons, i.e. beings who are rational, and thus capable of acting from duty.[15]

The second part of Pogge's alternative interpretation is in effect a reversal of the apparent relation of FUL and FH as it is given in Kant. He concludes from what he has said above that FH is not to be read in the light of FUL but that FUL is to be read in the light of FH:

B2 Rational beings must treat one another as ends in themselves, i.e. each must choose maxims so that all can contain or endorse them (even while the maxim's end remains attainable for him) [the rule of FH]. However, I may assume that all persons can endorse *my* adopting M if (and only if) they can endorse **M**'s adoption by any other person as well. In order to test M, I must therefore ask: *Can all persons endorse that M should be available to any person* (even while M's end remains attainable)? I cannot will M if it fails this test. [16]

This tendency to read FUL in the light of FH and thus to narrow the scope of the formula of universal law seems to be fairly widespread in modern Kant commentaries. Allen Wood, for example, speaking of Kant's distinction between "persons" and "things," is not completely unsympathetic to those who refuse to accept a distinction which treats nonrational beings as mere means. But he seems to believe that a correct analysis of FH necessarily leads to that conclusion:

> Once again, Kant's exclusionary claim [with respect to animals] can be made out only as a corollary of his positive argument that rational beings alone are to be regarded as ends in themselves.[17]

This seems to be the same contention that we have seen in Pogge. Wood is assuming that the status of "end in itself" rules out the possibility of treating nonrational sentients as objective ends in any sense at all.[18]

But in the light of what we have argued as the proper scope of Kant's second formulation, this restriction of FUL to humans cannot be justified. Animals are ends in themselves as much as humans; this is a necessary implication of *either* of the first two forms of the categorical imperative.

Pogge, to be sure, is right to say that FH, as he interprets it, would rule out maxims that seem to defeat Kant's intention in FUL by referring to a particular subset of persons. FH would require that we adopt no maxim that puts other humans at a disadvantage for our benefit. Hence a maxim discriminating against a particular subset of persons would have to be rejected because the members of that subset would be treated as a means.[19] Pogge sees no other way to avoid a problem that is seemingly inherent in FUL.

Nevertheless, we have already shown that Kant is assuming that any maxim presented to the test of FUL must already be universal in its form. He had no need of anything in FH to filter out maxims, presented for testing by FUL, which discriminate against a particular subset of subjects. Hence there is no reason not to regard FH, as Kant would formulate it, as another way of looking at FUL. By the same reasoning, there is nothing lost if FH is reformulated as FS, that is, in terms of sentience.

We may now pause for a moment to rule out a possible *reductio ad absurdum* of our basic position. We began with the maxim, "I eat the flesh of any animal I wish," and we categorically ruled that out because it points to cannibalism. Suppose we now adopt an even broader maxim: "I eat anything I like." If we universalize this maxim, it too will point to cannibalism. If we rule it out categorically, we will rule out vegetables as well, and so doom ourselves to death by starvation. Either we must include humans in a possible diet or we must abstain from food altogether. How, then, can we pursue the line of reasoning we have taken without going all the way from excluding animals as legitimate food to ruling out all possible nutrients, including vegetables, as things we can consume in good conscience?

The answer here requires distinguishing between the kinds of entities encompassed in the two maxims we have considered. Animals as well as humans can suffer pain, deprivation, and unwanted death. Vegetables cannot. Hence there is a very fundamental and relevant sense in which we cannot harm a vegetable. Anything we do to a head of lettuce or the bloom of a flower can be harmful (or beneficial) to one or more sentient beings who feed on these or otherwise enjoy them. The head of lettuce and the flower, however, feel nothing and regret nothing so far as we know. An exception for vegetables is thus consistent with the categorical imperative; an exception for humans with respect to eating animals is not.[20] Hence the second form of the categorical imperative remains FS, which is a reference to sentience. It does not require us to treat vegetables as ends in themselves.

I thus disagree with Tom Regan and others who would extend the idea of rights to cover not only vegetables but even inanimate objects. There is, Regan contends, a "goodness" in a good car that is independent of its utility or aesthetic interest for us. This much is plausible. But the argument is less plausible in citing this intrinsic goodness to establish the possibility "that mere things and plants *can* have rights."[21] The problem here arises from an ambiguity as to the meaning of "rights." If the basis of having a right is being good in some quasi-Platonic sense, Regan's point is at least arguable. But that route would require him to abandon his critique of perfectionism. He would have to agree that some goods can have more good in them than others, and can thus be better than others. Regan would then be bound to admit that, where need be, the lower good must be sacrificed to the higher. A well-formed pig is good and has a right to exist by virtue of that goodness. But if the smoke from a roasting pig serves to inspire a brilliant dissertation on cuisine, let it be served well-done!

On the other hand, if having a right has something to do with equality, the right of that pig to have its life and to enjoy it is valid against any human agent. That sacred right belongs to the pig as an entity that has sentience. Therefore, that right belongs to the pig as a subject, and not as an object in which some sort of goodness is present. The "goodness" of cars and vegetables as a claim to rights is thus diametrically opposed to Regan's own central doctrine of inherent value. He insists on the inherent value of the receptacle, not on the contents, as the criterion of moral value. For him, as for Kant, the ground of right is subjectivity. This is not to deny that things and plants can have immense value to human beings and to other animals as well. We may all agree that wanton destruction of a beautiful flower or a classic sculpture is a crime. But it is a crime against other human beings who love the objects, not a crime against the rose or the statue.

It thus appears that there is nothing in Kant thus far to justify his exclusion of animals from the scope of the categorical imperative. Animals cannot be excluded from the first formula except by an unjustified narrowing of its scope; they cannot be excluded from the second formula since the restriction to humanity cannot be rationally grounded. We shall also see later on that only in this perspective can the categorical imperative apply to human infants and mental defectives.

The Formula of Autonomy and the Kingdom of Ends

There are two additional formulations of the categorical imperative that need to be considered briefly. The formula of the kingdom of ends (FKE) is to act so that "the will can regard itself as at the same time making universal law by means of its maxim"; the formula of autonomy (FA) is the idea "of the will of every rational being as a will which makes universal law."[22] The point of FA is that we may regard ourselves as the very authors of the moral laws by which we are bound. According to FKE, furthermore, we participate with all other rational beings in creating a system of legislation. Both formulations of the categorical imperative thus refer to humans only. Humans and humans only, one would agree, not only make and execute the moral law, but they alone are also bound by it. The issue we have been considering, however, does not turn on the *source* of law, but rather on the scope of its protection. Hence neither of these further formulations affects our argument that the categorical imperative necessarily entails the duty of humans to respect the integrity of animals.

Animals, of course, cannot be members of the possible commonwealth envisaged by these rules. To put it in the simplest terms, they cannot have a right to vote even in imagination. But the meaning of the commonwealth, properly interpreted, is not merely a bond among its members. The commonwealth, as the first two forms of the categorical imperative now indicate, expresses the collective duty of humanity not only to create an order of harmony among themselves but also to do so between themselves on the one side and all sentient existences on the other as far as possible. They may even be required to promote harmony among nonhuman animals by mediating between them, but here too only so far as that is possible.

It might still be possible to "save" the exclusion of animals not by appeal to the idea of rational agency as in Kant, but by a direct intuition that only humans can have moral standing. But even this is hopeless. The intuition of a principle must withstand critical reflection in order to be validated. And the imagined intuition by which animals would be denied moral standing does not survive this test. Our prereflective judgment as human beings is that we ought not to inflict "unnecessary" or "avoidable" pain on animals. Animal rights theorists, of course, will not accept what is usually meant by "necessary" or "unavoidable."[23] But variations as to meaning notwithstanding, an intuition that humans can indeed inflict *unjustifiable* harm on animals means that there is at least some sense in which they have moral standing. If "wrong" can be done to animals, they must have rights. The restriction of moral standing to the human species would thus turn out to be a prejudice rather than a valid intuition.[24]

Questions of interpretation, of course, will inevitably arise as to what is meant by saying that animals have rights. What is the line, for example, between sentient and nonsentient? In what sense can domesticated animals be said to share in our ends? Are there any circumstances in which the right of the human species might have priority?[25] Some of these issues will be taken up in later chapters. But the basic implications of what has been argued thus far are clear enough. Animals cannot be eaten, made to serve for entertainment, used for biomedical experiments, etc.

I have thus tried to show that Kant's moral doctrine must either be rejected altogether or else its scope must be broadly interpreted as I have suggested. The obligation of the categorical imperative, although it is imposed on humans and other rational beings only, must apply to all sentients. Thus interpreted, Kant could well provide the conceptual foundation, as yet lacking, for the concept of inherent value. Regan himself, indeed, looks forward to a development of this sort:

> It might be thought—and it is thought by some, most notably Kant—for reasons explained in an earlier chapter (5.5)—that the notion of inherent value or some related idea (e.g. conceiving moral agents as "ends in themselves") applies to all moral agents and only to moral agents is arbitrary.[26]

Regan's judgment is correct, I believe. But it cannot be founded conceptually until the categorical imperative has been reinterpreted and revised.

Evelyn Pluhar offers a possible alternative to the Kantian idea of reason by founding the rights of animals on the rationalist moral theory of Alan Gewirth. The starting point for Gewirth is to show that every rational being who proposes to act must claim a right to freedom. But any human individual who (unavoidably) makes this claim in order to act must acknowledge that all other persons have this right as well:

> Now whatever the description under which or the sufficient reason for which it is claimed that a person has some right, the claimant must admit, on pain of contradiction, that this right also belongs to any other person to whom that description or sufficient reason applies. This necessity is an exemplification of the formal principle of universalizibility, which says that whatever is right for one person must be right for any similar person in similar circumstances.[27]

This is what Gewirth calls the "Principle of Generic Consistency" (PGC): *Act in accord with the generic rights of your recipients as well as of yourself.* And this distinguishes Gewirth's idea of rationalist universalism from Kant's. The categorical imperative works by imposing my maxim on all others as a universal law, and this, for Gewirth, is why one can manipulate the statement of his aims to justify a selfish end, the form of universalization notwithstanding. But PGC looks to the recipient of my prospective act. It requires that I acknowledge that any other person may claim the same right to freedom that I claim for myself. My maxim is not imposed on any other as though it were a law. Rather, the recipient of my intended action is now morally free, and it is within his or her right to consent to what I propose to do or not.[28]

Gewirth excludes animals, children, and the mentally deficient from all the benefits of his principle since "they lack for the most part the ability to control their behavior by unforced choice, to have knowledge of relevant circumstances beyond what is present to immediate awareness" (120). Animals must be given some consideration in proportion to their capacities, but not as much as what normal human beings can claim.

Pluhar disagrees. She sees no reason why this imperative should not work in favor of the very young, the mentally deficient, mammals, birds, and fish. As long as the entity is capable of conation, i.e., is consciously purposive, it should qualify under PGC. Indeed, even machines made by humans would qualify if they were "consciously purposive" and had "desires and initiative."[29]

Pluhar thus comes to much the same conclusions via Gewirth that we have come to via Kant, and she accepts all of Gewirth's rationalist universalism except for one correction. Various critics of Gewirth have noted an apparent equivocation in his use of the word "claim." He moves, they object, from the requirement that we acknowledge the right of others to *claim* a right of freedom by the rule of PGC, just as we did, to the conclusion that they *have* freedom. But there is no inherent guarantee that any claim to freedom will be recognized. Hence those who claim the right may not, as Gewirth believes, possess it.

Pluhar is very much aware of this objection, and on this point her defense of Gewirth seems adequate. What the prospective actor is really saying, and what he or she should have been more clearly represented as saying by Gewirth, is not: "I *claim* . . . rights" but rather "I *have* rights." For this is what the individual actually has in mind. In order to think of herself as a prospective actor she must believe she has the freedom and well-being to undertake it. Hence when *this* belief is generalized, it leads to a universal and categorical recognition of the right for all humans and also for the other sentient beings that Pluhar has in mind:

> Since the agent must hold that she has rights, by Gewirth's argument, not that she claims rights, the judgment to be universalized is "I [on the grounds that I am a prospective purposive agent] *have* the rights to freedom and well-being." The rest follows just as Gewirth has said. He is not guilty of equivocating "having a right" with "claiming a right." (248)

There is, however, a more serious, and indeed fatal, flaw in Gewirth's argument of which Pluhar seems unaware. When Gewirth insists that the prospective actor has to claim a right to freedom, he does not specify the scope of the freedom thus asserted. And without that particular specification, or else a general specification as to what is meant by "the right to freedom," the argument collapses. For if freedom (or the right to freedom) is a freedom to do everything one may wish or a right to take anything one can without limit, and if we are bound to recognize that right in all others as well, we are back at Hobbes' state of nature. In Hobbes too, individuals in a state of nature have a right to everything, and they too are bound to acknowledge that all others have that right as well. But these rights are inherently conflicting. The binding morality that Gewirth is seeking simply does not exist.

Or else we can say that freedom or the right to freedom is limited by respect for the rights of others. But that would bring us back to a law of nature which we and all others have a prior obligation to respect. But it is the very point of Gewirth's doctrine to avoid such antecedent obligation. For the law of nature is either the command of God as known to reason (as in Locke) or a synthetic *a priori* of practical reason (as in Kant). We might add that if appeal to the revealed or evident command of God is ruled out, then Kant alone is left.

I conclude that Kant's categorical imperative, in the revised form that I have given it, is a proper foundation for the theory of animal rights. Yet Kant's idea of a purely rational will is highly abstract, and it is not always easy to see how pure practical reason can determine our will without more in the way of motive or incentive. The usual motives—such as happiness or even hope in God and an afterlife—are ruled out as heteronomous. The only proper ground for Kant is reverence for law and satisfaction in performance of our duty. Hence his moral theory seems to depend in the last analysis on some variation of his critical idealism.

Doubts about the possibility of strict rationalism generally, and Kant's critical philosophy in particular, have led in recent years to a number of attempts to retain much of the force of Kant's ethics without its apparent difficulties. As a substitute for the categorical imperative, a fundamental contract on justice among humans is imagined, or else a dialogue among them that is fully open and productive. Theories like those of Rawls and Habermas also ignore, or lightly pass over, the interests of animals. I believe that with these doctrines, unlike Kant's, the exclusion of animals turns out to be a fatal weakness. The theories mentioned are founded neither on a transcendental idea of reason nor the necessities of a rational nature. They are constructed rather from the most generalized interests of a human community from which animals are excluded. They thus foreclose a vital consideration that is implied in Kant. When Kant's idea of universal law is carried to its logical conclusion, it can be made to cover the moral interests of other species as well as of humanity. But the theories of the post-Kantians I have mentioned are limited to strictly human interests by the very way in which they are derived. I shall try to show in the following chapter that they have no coherent and rational way of justifying this basic limitation.

4

Animal Rights and
Post-Kantian Rationalism

I have argued that Kant's strictly rationalist idea of universalization can be shown to require respect for animals, notwithstanding his own intention to exclude them. Kant's overall position is sometimes considered unacceptable because of his difficult theory of mind. But a number of philosophers, deeply attracted by the power of Kant's moral thought, have attempted to get roughly similar results from the logic of agreement among individuals seeking to reform the moral basis of their community. The problems in Kant are thereby bypassed. But new and perhaps even more insoluble problems arise from the denial, apparently inevitable in these theorists, of moral standing to animals.

With John Rawls, the universalization of rules—in his case the principles of justice—is achieved by the idea of a contract, or agreement, among participants in an "original position." Their conditions are hidden from them by a "veil of ignorance." They do not know their date of birth, sex, religious and other preferences, their social standing, or their skills and talents. They know only the general principles that govern social processes. Special circumstances are thus filtered out by the construction of the original position so that the preferences of the participants are purely general. Being ignorant of any special preferences or interests, they arrive at an "agreement about justice" that all are now committed to follow. The rules of justice are thus the functional equivalent of Kant's categorical imperative. The "veil of ignorance" and the "original position" offer a procedure for determining which principles of justice will be chosen with complete impartiality. It is a procedure that recommends itself to Rawls because it bypasses Kant's epistemological and metaphysical presuppositions, while avoiding the difficulties of utilitarianism.

On the exclusion of animals, Rawls is neither as dogmatic nor as harsh as Kant. Yet the outcome is ultimately the same. There are two places in *A Theory of Justice* where, albeit briefly, he raises the question of animals. The context for the first is a discussion of equality. "Here," says Rawls, "the meaning of equality is specified by:

> the principles of justice which require that equal basic rights be assigned to all persons. Presumably this excludes animals; they have some protection certainly but their status is not that of human beings. But this outcome is still unexplained. We have yet to consider what sorts of beings are owed the guarantees of justice. . . .
> The answer seems to be that it is precisely the moral persons who are entitled to equal justice. Moral persons are distinguished by two features: first they are capable of having (and are assumed to have) a conception of their good (as expressed by a rational plan of life); and second they are capable of having (and are assumed to acquire) a sense of justice, a normally effective desire to apply and to act on the principles of justice. We use the characterization of the persons in the original position to single out the kind of beings to whom the principles chosen apply.[1]

A few pages on, Rawls takes up the limits of a theory of justice:

> Not only are many aspects of morality left aside, but no account is given of right conduct in regard to animals and the rest of nature. A conception of justice is but one part of a moral view. While I have not maintained that the capacity for a sense of justice is necessary in order

to be owed the duties of justice, it does seem that we are not required to give strict justice anyway to creatures lacking this capacity. But it does not follow that there are no requirements at all in regard to them, nor in our relations with the natural order. Certainly it is wrong to be cruel to animals and the destruction of a whole species can be a great evil. The capacity for feelings of pleasure and pain and for the forms of life of which animals are capable clearly imposes duties of humanity and compassion in their case. I shall not attempt to explain these considered beliefs. They are outside the scope of a theory of justice, and it does not seem possible to extend the contract doctrine so as to include them in a natural way.[2]

These comments on the moral standing of animals are ambiguous and perhaps even equivocal.[3] It seems that Rawls is trying to combine two separate ideas into a single statement. One is an order of justice applicable only to humans and the other is the idea of an indirect duty to animals[4]. His attempt to meld the two is generous and civilized. Nonetheless, it is clear that animals are excluded from the original position and from the agreement about justice as strictly understood.

One usual response of animal rights theorists to Rawls, and indeed to Kant as well, is to press the difficulty of drawing a line between those who are moral agents and those who are not. Animals are clearly not moral agents because they cannot act by general moral principles. But mentally impaired humans and perhaps even human infants, according to this criticism, are not moral agents either; if they have moral standing, as we normally believe they do, why not animals as well? These critics hold that by denying equal moral standing to animals, Kant and Rawls must deny it to mentally disabled and undeveloped humans also. For the reasons given in our discussion of Kant, this outcome cannot be softened by appeal to some vague notion of indirect duty.

As Tom Regan sees it, this dilemma of the speciesist in handling marginal cases strengthens his point that all mammals of a year or more of age, no matter what their moral capacities, have equal claims to moral consideration.[5] They may not be moral agents, but they have rights nonetheless as moral patients. Although they cannot do injustice, they can suffer it. To deny this is to say that human moral patients are equally devoid of rights and that we have no obligations toward them.

This is an appealing argument in favor of acknowledging that animals have rights, and it appears very often in the literature supporting that position. But at least against Rawls, this argument would not suffice because he reluctantly accepts the consequences, or at least an important part of them. He cautiously disclaims any attempt to include mentally disabled humans any more than animals in his theory of justice. Equal justice is owed only to those "who have the capacity to take part in and to act in accordance with the public understanding of the initial situation."[6] Normal infants are moral persons because they are born with that capacity.[7] But mentally disabled humans who are permanently incapacitated are not included:

> The problem of those who have lost their realized capacity temporarily through misfortune, accident, or mental stress can be regarded in a similar way [to infants]. But those more or less permanently deprived of moral personality may present a difficulty. I cannot examine this problem here, but I assume that the account of equality would not be materially affected.[8]

Rawls sometimes speaks, albeit vaguely, of "natural duties" in *A Theory of Justice*, which might (or might not) be taken to mean that these form a special area of obligation apart from the duties of justice arising from the original position.[9] Neither interpretation, however, solves the problem of animals. If there is a real duty, and it arises from the original position, then their interests ought to have been considered in reaching an agreement on justice. But if there are duties to animals outside of the agreement about justice, which is thus to acknowledge that they have moral standing nonetheless, the failure to include them in the original position would be inconsistent. These and similar difficulties[10] may explain why Rawls makes no mention of natural duties in his later works *Political Liberalism*, *The Law of Peoples*, and *Justice as Fairness*.

The real problem in Rawls, then, is that the exclusion of animals and the disabled from the original position is never justified. He believes that some consideration is due to them and "to the rest of nature." But he sees no way of accounting for it within the theory of justice and can only hope that some solution to the problem will be found in the future.[11] That hope notwithstanding, Rawls's problem with the original position is much the same as Kant's in the categorical imperative. The restriction of participation to normal humans goes unjustified. The only advantage in Rawls is that he admits the difficulty.

The issue, however, cannot be postponed. If it is agreed that recognition of rights in animals is a rational duty, how can these rights be overridden without just cause? And how can we determine what a just cause would be without including animals in the original position and the agreement about justice?

In *Political Liberalism* Rawls answers, in effect, that his theory does not deal with all of justice, to say nothing of general morality, but only with "political justice." This entitles him, he claims, to avoid any comprehensive theory. He will merely examine what follows for social institutions and personal attitudes from the idea of normal human beings participating in a fair system of cooperation. The rule of his "political constructivism" is that many moral issues can be left to more truly comprehensive theories so long as these exhibit an overlapping consensus on those areas that are covered by political justice.[12]

There seem to be at least two kinds of issues that this doctrine must accommodate. One is the resolution of such questions as the legitimacy of using nuclear weapons or of capital punishment. These are not covered by political justice, but in a well-ordered democracy partisans will not deem them worth a conflict severe enough to undermine the democratic political order that political justice sanctions.[13] Adherents of different comprehensive theories, religious or otherwise, may come to conflicting positions. These, however, are to be treated as reasonable disagreements outside the scope of political justice.

But there is a second, and less manageable, issue to which political justice would have to accommodate. This one has to do with such questions as charity to the disabled and the treatment of animals. These are barely mentioned in *A Theory of Justice* and seem to have been passed over entirely in *Political Justice*. They are, however, extremely difficult to handle within the bounds of political constructivism. Charity toward the mentally disabled, and others incapable of productive participation in society, is not a controversial question. It is espoused by virtually every religion and is all but universally approved by the public. Yet Rawls has no choice but to exclude charity from political justice since political constructivism deals only with normal human beings in a fair system of social cooperation. Rawls, as we have seen, would very much like to see his theory extended to encompass charity. But he cannot find a way to do so, and indeed no way seems logically possible.

The question of animal rights is no doubt more controversial in public opinion than charity toward defective humans. But here too, as we have already noted, there is a public consensus that animals should not be subjected to unnecessary or avoidable pain, a sentiment more or less embodied in public law. This view implies that animals have rights. These rights may be taken as limited or extensive, but in either case the exclusion of animals from the original position and political justice requires justification in a way that the issues of nuclear arms and capital punishment do not. The latter policies raise questions of degree—of more or less destruction, more or less punishment—that are admittedly difficult and even highly charged. But the moral standing of potential enemies and convicted criminals is not in question. The question with animals, on the other hand, is whether they are entities which, by their inherent nature, are to be included in political justice. That is more fundamental, at least logically, than a choice of policies; it is, in other words, a question of moral standing. It is intuitively clear that animals as well as disabled humans have moral standing and are the subjects of rights in one degree or another.

Animals and the disabled can thus be victims of injustice and must be included in the original position. To accomplish this, the entities who participate must not know what species they belong to.

What happens, then, when the veil of ignorance, thus universalized, is lifted? Regan spells out the consequences with devastating force. There is no principled reason, he shows, why participants should be assured that they will turn out to be normal humans when the veil is lifted. They must thus take the obvious precautions. Since they can imagine incarnation as mentally disabled humans, they will select principles of justice protective of that interest. By the same reasoning they will want to protect the interests of nonhuman animals. Nor can this outcome be precluded by raising metaphysical objections to the possibility of incarnation as an animal. "To allow those in the original position to know what *species* they will belong to is to allow them knowledge no different in kind from allowing them to know what race or sex they will be."[14] Hence attempts to raise metaphysical objections to the possibility of incarnation as animals are bound to fail on Rawls's premises about identity.[15] Rawls himself strongly insists in *Political Liberalism* that the "veil of ignorance has no specific metaphysical implications concerning the nature of the self."[16] And much as he deplores its consequences, Peter Carruthers, one of Regan's most determined critics, feels obliged to admit the logic of Regan's critique of Rawls on the veil of ignorance. The veil of ignorance would not require that animals appear in the original position as beings without the capacity to reason. Their interests are rather to be embraced by disembodied rational agents. "For it is presumably possible," says Carruthers, "that rational agents

> should bracket their status as rational agents, even in the process of rationally constructing a system of rules. If they can forbear from making use of their knowledge of their sex and social status, then presumably they can just as well forbear from making use of their knowledge of their species or, indeed, of the fact that they are rational agents.[17]

What, then, would the agreement on justice include if the possibility of incarnation as an animal were introduced into an expanded construction of the original position? Very little is the inevitable answer. The determination of what rules of distribution will bring about the best position of that class of society which is the worst off—that is, the difference principle—would no longer be relevant. One cannot speak of the "advantages" of animals generically, or talk about the maximin conditions of the great variety of species that would have to be considered. A commentator who supports Regan suggests, instead, a "decent existence" as the common principle of justice.[18] But this measure could hardly be the same for all species. A decent existence for zebras would mean, among other policies, eliminating lions, while a decent existence for lions would require making zebras more available.

There thus appears to be only one basic claim that all species would have in common. They would all agree that no animal, human or nonhuman, should be treated as an instrument by humans. This does not require us to say that it is "unjust" for one nonhuman animal to eat another. The rule of justice is binding only on normal human beings, and only they, as moral agents, can do injustice to each other, and also to animals as moral patients. Where, then, the representation of animal interests is included in the original position, the outcome is essentially the same as in the revised version of the second form of the categorical imperative offered earlier. Sentient beings must never be treated only as a means. Nothing else, and especially not the difference principle, would be part of the basic agreement. Rules of property, of contract, and of the redistribution of product would become relevant only when the veil of ignorance is lifted and systems of conscious cooperation are instituted. These will consist primarily of relations among human beings. But insofar as domesticated animals enter into human systems of cooperation, concern for their well-being and (ascribed) interest in cooperating with humans will also be obligatory upon their human custodians and partners.

Revision of the original position to accommodate the rights of animals would thus undermine its function in Rawls's theory of justice. Peter Carruthers acknowledges that this would be the outcome, but somehow manages to conclude that it is not Rawls who is at fault but Regan! "The real line of reply to Regan," he says, "is that his suggestion would destroy the theoretical coherence of Rawls's contractualism. As Rawls has it, morality is, in fact, a human construction. . . . To suggest, now, that contractualism should be so construed as to accord equal moral standing to animals would be to lose our grip on where moral notions are supposed to come from, or why we should care about them when they arrive.[19]

Carruthers here is right about the consequences, but wrong about the remedy. The consequences of Regan's criticism of Rawls cannot be shown to be wrong theoretically, nor can they be set aside simply because they may be theoretically inconvenient.

Hence just as Kant's version of the categorical imperative is no longer the basic ground of ethics once it is properly universalized, so also with the revised original position of Rawls. That procedure too is meant to establish universal principles abstracted from every private interest of the participants. It turns out, however, that the yield from political justice is far less than expected when a proper view of moral standing is introduced. It does not issue in a theory of equal opportunity and distributive justice, but in the simple finding that no sentient being may be treated as a mere instrument. This is to make Rawls's procedure redundant. The right of animals is already implied in recognizing that animals have moral standing. Indeed, the idea that animals may not be harmed without just cause is precisely what is meant by saying that they have moral standing. Yet the construction of the original position in a satisfactory form presupposes, as we have seen, this recognition of animals. The rights of humans, of course, are more extensive than the rights of animals; they include the basic rights associated with the capacity to reason. But that does not affect the fundamental claim of animals to equal respect on matters of equal relevance. The sole result of the original position is that sentient beings must never be treated as mere means.

This rule does not necessarily imply that all sentient beings must also be treated as ends under all circumstances, in the sense that they are always entitled to human intervention on their behalf. There are conditions in which one may be bound to intervene against abuse of animals by humans. But against nature the ability to help is rare. Wild animals are an obvious example. They can be used, illicitly, as instruments in many ways, such as hunting, trapping, and most forms of captivity in zoos. But enhancement of their well-being in the wild is rarely obligatory for humans. Under most circumstances we cannot sensibly mediate between predator and prey or adjust a given species to an alteration in its food supply. Such interventions are normally beyond our powers, given some reasonable schedule of priorities.

Concern for the well-being of animals becomes mandatory only when they become participants in a scheme of cooperation instituted by humans. Here too, however, there is a difference between animals and humans in what it means to treat an individual as an end. Something like the "difference" principle still applies to moral agents in that cooperation by human beings ought to be rewarded with equal benefits except insofar as differences enhance the well-being of the least advantaged. This rule need not be based on the principle of fairness as it is found in Rawls. Rather it may be derived from the rationally grounded rule forbidding exploitation. Cooperation among humans is a group affair instituted for the common good of all. If some participants are left worse off than they could be if redistribution were instituted, they are being exploited as means, at least to some degree.

Some animals may also be considered as participants with humans in a cooperative enterprise. With modern technology this class continually shrinks. But one could say that cows participate in milk production; that cats, dogs, and horses serve as pets; and that primates sometimes take part in learning and speech experiments. Under present conditions much of this "participation" is in the form of brutal exploitation. But I am thinking here of ideal possibilities in a profoundly reformed society. If the services mentioned above are not onerous, and if they are rewarded by a comfortable existence over a whole lifetime, the participation of animals could perhaps be considered as "virtually" voluntary. Their welfare needs, no doubt, are relatively fixed, and their share per capita of the social product would not increase by much with increased productivity. But they would not be victims of exploitation and would in a sense receive equal consideration, relative to their natures, as ends. The same kind of reasoning, we might note, would apply to mentally disabled humans as well.

Universalizability is also central to the moral theory of Jürgen Habermas. He comes to this fundamentally Kantian idea not from analytic philosophy as does Rawls, but rather from the school of critical theory which has its roots in Hegel and Marx. But for Habermas too the Kantian idea, suitably reworked, is central to the construction of a moral theory. The restatement, as it were, of Kant by Rawls is by use of the device of the original position to achieve impartiality. For Habermas, on the other hand, the reconstruction is given by the notion of "an ideal speech situation."

The fatal weakness of the categorical imperative for Habermas is that it is arrived at by an internal monologue rather than a real exchange of views, and also that it is abstracted from all existing social and cultural conditions. For Kant the reflections through which moral rules are established occur only within the mind of every individual and are then considered to be applicable universally without regard to the concrete historical conditions under which they have to be applied.

For Habermas, all assertions claiming truth have to be redeemed in actual discourse. Scientific hypotheses are redeemed by common interpretations of the experimental evidence. Moral assertions are no less cognitive and no less capable of being proven true. But the discursive method appropriate to morals is unique. Claims to validity must be validated by the participation of everyone affected in a process of practical reasoning, or argument:

> A norm cannot be considered the common interest of all who are affected simply because it seems acceptable to some of them under the condition that it be applied in a non-discriminatory fashion. The intuition expressed in the idea of the generalization of maxims intends something more than this, namely that valid norms must

deserve recognition by *all* concerned. It is not sufficient, therefore, for *one person* to will the adoption of a contested norm after considering the side effects and the consequences that would occur if all persons followed that norm or whether every person in an identical position could will the adoption of such a norm. In both cases the process of judging is relative to the vantage point and perspective of *some* and not *all* concerned. . . . Thus every valid norm has to fulfill the following condition:

(U) *All* affected can accept the consequences and the side effects its *general* observance can be anticipated to have for the satisfaction of *everyone's* interests (and these consequences are preferred to those of known alternative possibilities for regulation).

We should not mistake this principle of universalization (U) for the following principle, which already contains the distinctive idea of an ethics of discourse.

(D) Only those norms can claim to be valid that meet (or could meet) with the approval of all affected in their capacity *as participants in a practical discourse.*[20]

Three additional considerations might be cited to help make this procedure clearer. Practical discourse (a discussion about goals and aims) is to be understood as being conducted in the light of an "ideal speech situation." This means, first, that all who can speak competently can participate, that all expressions of attitude and questionings are permitted, and that all coercion is ruled out except the force of the better argument.[21] But second, this does not mean that the ideal speech situation is present, imminent, or even fully possible. It is rather something to be anticipated when norms are to be validated. "It is clear enough," writes William Outhwaite, "that Habermas never intended the ideal speech situation to be understood as a concrete utopia which would turn the world into a gigantic seminar."[22] Third, the requirement of validation does not mean that all working norms have been or ought to be validated by the above procedure. Human individuals exist in a given nexus of immediately understood and mostly unarticulated norms and understanding that Habermas calls "the lifeworld." There is always "the horizon of unquestioned, intersubjectively shared, non-thematized certitude that participants in communication have 'at their backs.'"[23] Only when this lifeworld is challenged or disrupted must new norms or amendments of old ones be consciously considered for possible validation.

Animals obviously cannot be included in an ideal speech situation, whether it be actual or anticipated. The whole idea of a discourse ethic, of the acceptance of new norms through dialogue, makes it clear that animals are excluded from the process. But Habermas, as far as I am aware, makes no attempt to justify this exclusion, and I believe that no justification is possible that would be consistent with his basic point of view. Even if one were to allow humans to represent animal species, the difficulties would be pretty much the same as those encountered with Rawls. Needs and aims differ with each species. We might attempt to avoid this difficulty by permitting humans of good will to agree on norms that would govern the treatment of animals by humans. But this surely seems to violate the basic principle of a discourse ethic. It is, in principle, monological so far as the animals are concerned. And if monologue is adopted, one is back with Kant and all the difficulties associated with his moral theory.

There is one other contractual theory, sketched in outline, the failure of which can help to illustrate even further the deep dilemma attendant on all of them. Onora O'Neill, a leading commentator on Kant's moral theory, holds that Kant's position does not ultimately depend on metaphysics. His idea of reason in *The Critique of Pure Reason*, she tries to show, need not be derived from the *a priori* conditions of objective knowledge. It follows rather from the logic of what it is that makes communication possible among a plurality of potentially rational individuals. Beings like ourselves

> without prescribed modes of coordination . . . cannot share a world if there is no cognitive order. . . . The most then that they can do is to reject basic principles of thought and action that are barriers to cognitive order. . . . Those who are to be fellow workers must at least refrain from basing their action on basic principles that others cannot share. . . . [I]f they wholly reject [this step], communication and

interaction (even hostile interaction, let alone coordination) will be impossible. To act on this maxim is simply to make what Kant elsewhere calls the Categorical Imperative the fundamental principle of reasoning and acting. It is to base action and thought only on maxims which one can at the same time will that they be universal laws. [24]

O'Neill would thus justify a wholly revised conception of Kant's enterprise, not only in the *Groundwork* but also in his theory of knowledge. "The deep structure of the *Critique of Pure Reason* and the view of philosophic method that it exemplifies are both antirationalist and antifoundationalist" (4).

What O'Neill means by "deep structure" and universal laws in this antifoundationalist interpretation of Kant is indicated by her critique of Rawls. She is not dissatisfied with Rawls's basic project. But she finds his moral construct too closely tied to a particular culture. She criticizes him for having introduced a Western liberal ideal of personality in constructing his theory of justice. O'Neill then anticipates a universal agreement that is more abstract and so more readily reconciled with Kant:

> A more Kantian constructivism (perhaps not one everybody would attribute to Kant) must then start from the *least determinate* conceptions both of the rationality and of the mutual independence of agents.
>
> A meagre and indeterminate view of rationality might credit agents only with the capacity to understand and follow *some* form of social life, and with a commitment to seek *some* means to any ends (desired or otherwise) to which they are committed. (212)

Although O'Neill's idea of rationality is extremely abstract, it does not fall "foul of Mill's old charge" that Kant fails to derive any actual principles of duty. From an animal rights point of view it is instead much too narrow in confining itself as it does to human interests. She, like the others just surveyed, would construct the principles of moral reasoning by postulating a structure of human society upon which all agree, rather than deriving the structure of society from reason. Animals must thus be excluded, and that flaw, as I have tried to show, is fatal. Moral reason may be evoked by social development as Kant's anthropology indicates. But it does not determine reason's content or mode of acting on us.

It is perhaps a matter of sheer historical interest to note that there was at least one writer of the French Enlightenment who was acutely aware of animal rights as a problem. The insight here belongs not to Rousseau but to Diderot. Rousseau laments the plight of animals in human hands; he condemns the eating of animal flesh as unnatural and quotes Plutarch and Porphyry at length.[25] But he adds nothing of theoretical interest. Diderot, on the other hand, goes deeper, and his article on the general will in the *Encyclopédie* is especially instructive for present purposes because he confronts the fact that animals do not participate in forming it.

It is not clear whether it was Diderot or Rousseau who first introduced the idea of a general will to explain political obligation. But their sense of its scope is significantly different. In Rousseau the general will almost always refers to the internal cohesion of a state, that is to the obligations of the citizen. With Diderot the general will is more inclusively universalized:

> It is to the general will (*volonté générale*) that the individual should look to know what it means to be a man, a citizen, a subject, a father, a child and when it is right for him to live or to die. It is for the general will to determine the bounds of all his duties. You have a *natural right* (*droit naturel*) to anything that is not denied you by the entire race. It is in humanity that you will find the meaning of your thoughts and your desires.
>
> If you pay heed to what has been said above, you will always be convinced: . . . that a man who listens only to his particular will is an enemy to the human race; that the general will in each individual is a pure act of the understanding, which, the passions silent, reflects on what a man can demand from others like himself and what others may rightly demand of him.[26]

This universalist conception of the general will quite naturally leads Diderot to ask about duties between humanity and animals:

> Particular wills are suspect; they may be either good or bad; but the general will is always good; it never has deceived and never will deceive. If animals were on a level more or less equal to ours; if there were reliable means of communication between them and us; if they could clearly transmit their thoughts and sentiments to us and recognize ours with the same clarity; in a word, if they could vote in a general assembly, they would have to be called to attend, and the case for natural right would no longer be put before *humanity*, but before *animality*. But animals are separated from us by unchangeable and eternal barriers; and we are concerned here with a set of findings and ideas which are peculiar to the human species and which emanate from and constitute its dignity. (431–432)

Diderot is in error here, and the form of his mistake is paradigmatic for all the theorists we have discussed up to now. He assumes that animals, if they do not fit the conditions of moral agency, may be simply left out, and the obligations of morality confined to human beings. He fails to consider that there is something speciesist about that solution. He cannot and does not deny that animals have some sort of moral status. He should, therefore, have said that if animals cannot be included in the general will, there is something fundamentally wrong with that conception.

The fact that sentient beings cannot be taken as mere things is thus fatal to any theory that constructs morality on the outcome of some universal agreement among rational beings. Animals cannot take part, or even be represented, in any process of agreement, real or hypothetical. Even O'Neill's highly abstract agreement on morals does not, as we have seen, remove the difficulty arising from the failure to recognize animals as moral patients.

There is also a whole family of theories, going back to the ancients and revived by Hobbes and Hume, that are contractual or quasi-contractual in that they derive the obligation to do justly from enlightened self-interest. Unless all or most of us agree that we must treat each other according to the usual rules of justice, society as a whole will suffer and we will suffer with it. On this derivation of our obligations, we can have no duty toward animals and animals can have no claim to the benefits of justice. Humans may love animals and take good care of them, they may even be vegetarians, and there may well be agreements between one human and another by which animals are made to benefit. But animals cannot be parties to a binding agreement. They may share the same end momentarily but they cannot have any understanding with us that resembles a contract.[27]

Jan Narveson believes that an indirect obligation to animals can be established through the interests that humans have in them.[28] I do not want my pet, my child, or my mentally impaired aunt to be injured, and so I oppose injuring anyone in that class; I oppose infanticide of deformed children since I might have been born deformed. Not everybody, however, cares about pets, children, and aunts, and at this stage of life none of us can become the victims of infanticide.[29] Hence many people may not share, and will not be obliged to share, our protective attitudes, and no rule against these evils will be generally acknowledged.

This is perhaps the most likely place to include some remarks about Peter Carruthers's view of morals. He is aware, as we have seen, that he must offer a point of view that is consistent with his denial of equal respect for animals. In his book *The Animals Issue* he does not spell out his position in detail. But he does offer a version of contractualism, unfortunately much abbreviated, as an alternative to both Singer's utilitarian defense of animals and Regan's theory of animal rights. He would have a moral theory

> where the basic contractualist concept (as well as the desire to comply with it) is held to be innate, selected for in evolution because of its value in promoting the survival of our species.

It may be objected that this line of reply to Regan implausibly reduces morality to anthropology. But in fact it does no such thing. My claim is not that moral statements are really disguised claims about the conditions for the survival of the species. On the contrary, they are about what rational agents should reasonably accept who share the aim of reaching free and unforced agreement. My claim is only that we have this concept of morality innately, and have an innate desire to justify our actions in terms that others may freely accept, because doing so has promoted the survival of our species in the past. But if the contractualist concept expresses what morality *is*, for us, then there is no moral standpoint from which it can be criticized, or from which it can be argued that we are morally required to extend that concept so as to accord equal moral standing to animals.[30]

This sounds very much like an adaptation of Thomas Scanlon's version of contractualism, with some extra assumptions added to make it work. The problem in Scanlon is how we can all want to reach reasonable agreement, how we know what reasonable is, and why we are bound by it. For Carruthers the answers are simple. The desire is innate, and what is reasonable is what promotes survival of the species, assuming we can all agree on what that is. All of this is obscure enough. Why we are bound is even more obscure. Carruthers says that it is because the sense of being obliged is also innate, or because we necessarily care about the future of the species. What, then, is an "innate desire"? Is it an instinct, an idea, or what? And suppose we should disagree about what will advance the survival of the whole species now or in the long run. Or suppose that in any event, it is a goal to which we resist sacrificing our interests to achieve. The good of the species, after all, is not always coincident with our own self-interest except in the very long run that we will never live to see.[31]

For Carruthers, moral behavior is ultimately anthropology despite his protest to the contrary, just as moral behavior ultimately becomes social psychology for Narveson. Within the limits of these disciplines, some part of what they say might perhaps make sense. But neither of their positions can be called "philosophy." With Rawls and Habermas as well, and especially in the latter, there is much appeal to social processes antecedent to reflections on justice. But their arguments on justice and morality properly belong to philosophy. The agreements they postulate are compelled by logic, not recommended by prudence.

If we remain with philosophy, the fact that sentient beings cannot be taken as mere things proves fatal to any moral theory founded on some universal agreement among rational beings.

How, then, can a comprehensive account of human obligations toward each other and toward animals be developed? I would answer that the limitations of the post-Kantian theories we have been considering do not rule out a rational construction of morality. Unlike the post-Kantians, we must begin with a basic norm that antedates the hypothetical inauguration of society. In all the classical versions of the social contract the state of nature is governed by some such rule. In Grotius it is God's rational will. In Pufendorf and Locke it is the will of God. In Kant it is the categorical imperative itself. Part I of *The Metaphysics of Morals* shows how the categorical imperative is externalized in relations among humans, first as Private Right and then as Public Right. Mutatis mutandis, Kant's procedure is much like Locke's, except that Kant's views on public right are marred by his conservative prejudices. He rejects, inconsistently, any right of revolution not only by the individual but by the community as a whole. The way in which our present findings on animal rights would fit into a version of the social contract revised according to such principles might therefore be more easily imagined in the light of Locke.

The first and deeper level of Locke's *Second Treatise of Government* comprises the basic rights and corresponding duties that follow from the law of nature. This law, for Locke, derives from God's desire to preserve his handiwork. It thus requires a proof of God's existence which is no longer deemed possible by most philosophers. But Locke's belief in God as the ultimate author of the moral law that already governs in the state of nature can be replaced by the second form of Kant's categorical imperative (understood as we have amended it). This imperative, accordingly, would be the first, deeper level of Locke's account of moral obligation.

The second level is Locke's social contract. Neither here nor in the first level, or state of nature, do animals have duties. Locke, unfortunately, goes further, and falls into an error characteristic of his age. He would exclude animals not only from the human duties associated with the law of nature but also from any of the rights that it confers. God, he argues, must have intended humans to survive, and so they are permitted to go to nature for their food. This requires God's implied permission because nature is his creation and his property. This permission to use nature applies only to those parts of it that are clearly intended for that purpose. Since humans are created roughly equal to one another, it is clearly not God's intention that one human use another merely as a means. Humans must rather be respected and, if possible, preserved, in their existence and freedom. But all other animals, being "lower" than humans, may be exploited for food and other purposes. Just as animals (as well as humans) make use of vegetables, so humans may make use of animals.

Locke's line between life that is sacrosanct and life that is not thus corresponds not to sentience but to level of worth in a hierarchy of nature. His justification of eating the flesh of animals, together with the other uses this implies, is reminiscent of Aristotle. Yet Locke's epistemology is not Aristotelian, and neither is his natural theology. Like Pufendorf, and perhaps most of the more notable natural law theorists of the time, Locke is a voluntarist in theology, not an intellectualist. He does not hold, with the Thomists and neo-Thomists, that God was bound by reason in his creation of the universe, but rather that the creation is the expression of his will. That will must no doubt be good by its very nature and, having been promulgated, will not be changed.[32] But God's commands to humanity cannot be found by rational speculation about some portion of an eternal reason inherent in God's mind. His will can be ascertained only by empirical inspection of how nature has been constituted; this, indeed, is how Locke gets to the basic equality of humans and the inferiority of animals:

> A [natural] *State* also of *Equality*, wherein all the Power and Jurisdiction is reciprocal, no one having more than another: there being nothing more evident, than that Creatures of the same species and rank promiscuously born to all the same advantages of Nature, and the use of the same faculties, should also be equal one amongst another without Subordination or Subjection, unless the Lord and Master of them all, should by any manifest declaration of his Will set one above another, and confer upon him by clear appointment and undoubted Right to Dominion and Sovereignty.[33]

Two paragraphs later the meaning for animals is spelled out.

> "[T]here cannot be supposed any such *Subordination* among us, that may Authorize us to destroy one another, as if we were made for one anothers uses, as the inferior ranks of Creatures are for ours." (PAR. 6)

That animals are inferior to humans in many respects is indeed evident. But to go from this fact to the use of them as instruments, on the grounds that eating an animal is some sort of "nobler use, than its bare Preservation" is sheer speciesism. Locke could just as well have started from the status, common to animals and humans as sentient beings, and arrived at vegetarianism. God, after all, provided plenty of vegetables for humans to eat.

Suppose we substitute the idea of the categorical imperative, amended as suggested, to replace Locke's speciesist account of the law of nature. It now states that no sentient being shall ever be treated solely as a means but also at the same time as an end. The obligations of moral agents to respect life are not now restricted to other moral agents; they would also extend to animals as moral patients. Animals, in other words, would have the same presumptive right to life and liberty that humans have. It is perhaps too much to say that they also have a right to property even in the primitive sense of a right of access to the fruits of nature. All species, including the human species, are, or can be, in competition for the use of nature—a domain in which otherwise legitimate interests can come into conflict. The adjudication of possible conflicts between humans and other animal species is thus a problem in itself which I propose to treat later on in the chapter on environmentalism. Here I need only remark that the settlement of priorities between species would set the boundaries to the rights of any individual.

What I have said so far is consistent with the idea of a social contract among humans. The rights of animals do not bar humans from agreeing to form a government in which only they participate. But this does not abolish human duties to moral patients; it must instead be a way of enforcing them. Hence at every level of the formation of government, the relevant rights of animals must be expressly stated. The establishment of a constitution provides a good example. Animals could not be guaranteed freedom of speech or of the press. But any due process requirement would have to be written in terms of sentient beings, not persons in the human sense only. Consistent with the reformulated law of nature, every animal would have to be given a guarantee of representation in the courts by friendly humans.

There is an important clarification to be noted in comparing this formulation of the social contract with Locke's. In Locke the creation of government is almost always presented as a means of protecting and preserving the rights of one individual against infringement by another. In the formulation just proposed the emphasis falls on the enforcement of duties. Up to a certain point there is no difference between the two approaches. The rights of a human individual suppose a duty in others to respect them. Hence if government protects, it at the same time enforces the duty, so there is no particular need to emphasize the latter. With animals, though, the emphasis must shift since their rights are best understood as the consequence of human duties. The change to government established by means of the social contract, therefore, must also emphasize the enforcement of human duties.

The lack of symmetry between rights and duties for animals is not completely unfavorable to humankind. The extra burden thus placed on humans, who alone have duties as well as rights, has a certain compensation. Only they can participate in government.

One other approach to justice, to which we have alluded above, is prudentialism in its various forms. All such theories ultimately reduce to a conception of utility. For Hobbes the individual's own advantage is always paramount; this makes any genuine political obligation impossible. For Hume the individual supports a common good on which his own depends. But this common good is implicitly utilitarian, with all its larger difficulties. In any event, neither these nor any other form of prudentialism does full justice to the claims of animals.

We may conclude, therefore, that the rule against using any sentient being as a mere instrument for human advantage must be taken as the ultimate foundation of a theory of justice. Otherwise one must deny that justice is a virtue and substitute something like power as the highest good.

5

Animal Rights and Compassion

Kant famously holds that "It is impossible to conceive anything at all in the world, or even out of it, which can be taken as good without qualification except a *good will*."[1] A few paragraphs later the good will is identified with pure practical reason:

> [Reason's] true function is to produce a *will* which is *good*, not as a *means* to some further end, but *in itself* ... Such a will need not on this account be the sole and complete good, but it must be the highest good and the condition of all the rest, even of all our demands for happiness. (64)

For Kant, therefore, nothing but action for the sake of law, that is, from duty, has moral worth:

> To help others where one can is a duty, and besides this there are many spirits of so sympathetic a temper that, without any further motive of vanity or self-interest, they find an inner pleasure in spreading happiness around them and can take delight in the contentment of others as their own work. Yet I maintain that in such a case an action of this kind, however right and however amiable it may be, has still no genuinely moral worth. It stands on the same footing as other inclina-

tions . . . [since] its maxim lacks moral content, namely, the performance of such actions, not from inclination, but from *duty*.   (66)

This insistence on rationality, or duty, for its own sake, leads
some commentators to reject Kant's moral theory as too abstract, or
even empty. I do not accept that criticism. To act from and for the
moral imperative (on those all too rare occasions when one does),
generates a complex but strong experience. There is an inward glow
of rightness, strength, and justification. Outwardly, there is a special sense of connection and unity with the immediate object of the
will which at the same time extends outward without limitation.

The good will, in other words, is a well-being felt within one's self
for following the law, no matter what the occasion or the immediate
object of the act, and indeed no matter what the sacrifice. Con-
versely, failure to follow it is felt as a deficiency within us, and failure of others to follow it is felt by us as compassion for the victim of
the failure and indignation directed against the individual(s) who
shirked their duty.

Nevertheless, some writers have attempted to overcome and dispense with the moral imperative of reason by taking compassion as
the ultimate foundation of morality. By compassion is meant the
capacity to share the suffering of others and hope for its removal, or
to share the joy of others and hope to see it last. A fundamental condition for compassion as a moral principle, however, is some degree
of innocence in the object of the compassionate act. We are appro-
priately moved by the suffering of others only in so far as they are
innocent victims of misfortune or injustice. And we share the joy of
others only insofar as it results from merit or good fortune. Compassion for a murderer may be commendable, because of his or her
deprived childhood or abusive conditions of imprisonment. Happiness in the ill-gotten joy of a successful swindler is not. Thus qualified, compassion is a powerful force in support of animal rights.

Hence compassion cannot serve as an independent and sufficient
ground of rights for animals, or indeed for humans either. All
attempts to take it as foundational fail theoretically because, by their

very nature, such theories lack a principle for determining the innocence of the objects to which compassion should apply.

Perhaps the most celebrated of such theories is Albert Schweitzer's appeal to "reverence for life." According to Schweitzer, ethics is reverence for the "will to live," which is present in every sentient being:

> [Just] as in my own will-to-live there is a longing for wider life and for the mysterious exaltation of the will-to-live which we call pleasure, with dread of annihilation and of the mysterious encroachment on the will-to-live which we call pain; so is it also in the will-to-live all around me, whether it can express itself before me, or remains dumb.
>
> Ethics consist, therefore, in my experiencing the compulsion to show to all will-to-live the same reverence as I do to my own. There we have given us that basic principle of the moral which is a necessity of thought: It is good to maintain and promote life; it is bad to destroy life or obstruct it.[2]

By no means does Schweitzer think that the natural world is, or ever will be, peaceful and harmonious. "The world is a ghastly drama of will-to-live divided against itself. One existence makes its way at the cost of another; one destroys another" (249). But that cannot be a basis for resigned inaction. There is a longing in humanity for the will-to-live "to arrive at unity with itself, to become universal" (249).

This aspiration to unity in Schweitzer is avowedly mystical and quasi-religious. In itself this does not diminish the force of his idea; in some respects it enhances it. The real problem is that it leaves "reverence for life" and its associated ethic without the possibility of rational articulation. It defies reduction to or limitation by a rule:

> In ethical conflicts man can arrive only at subjective decisions. No one can lay down for him at what point, on each occasion, lies the extreme limit of possibility for his persistence in the preservation and promotion of life. He alone has to decide, by letting himself be guided by a feeling of the highest possible responsibility to other life. (255–256)

This appeal to feeling as the ultimate test is moving. But it does not help us make difficult choices; worst of all, it does not enable us to reach agreement. Two truly compassionate people can come to opposed intuitions about what to do in a given situation. Which of two contending embodiments of the will to live will they support? How much effort shall be expended in helping this one here rather than that one there? Rules of reason, therefore, are indispensable for deciding conflicts and avoiding bizarre applications of compassionate feelings.

The lack of a rule of reason to regulate compassion is also a serious objection to the ecofeminist "ethic of care." This approach rejects any priority for justice and rights in making ethical choices. Feminist in its modern origins, it attacks the very idea of rights as an ideological illusion engendered in the Western tradition by a long history of male domination, and it envisages a full and liberating replacement of that tradition by an "ethic of care."[3] Some of its proponents salute as forerunners several male philosophers from Shaftesbury to Max Scheler and Martin Buber, among others. But the new ethic supposedly could not have reached fruition were it not for feminism. Since women have borne the burden of repression throughout history, it is feminists who are supposedly best positioned to counter the logic of repression.[4]

Hence the strict morality of rights, although well intentioned, is said to be poisoned by the ethos of domination, which is latent in the very appeal to abstract rules of justice. A good human being should act instead only from loving attention to particular individuals in concrete contexts.[5] To understand the other, to know what the other really is, depends on sympathy, not abstract location in a class of objects. Abstract intellectualization screens out sympathy, and always cloaks oppression in one form or another.

The *bête noire* for proponents of the care ethic is inevitably Kant. The Kantian insistence that all action to be truly moral must come only from respect for the law, and not be based on feeling, seems to rule sympathy and care out of ethics altogether. Regan, although a rights proponent, is grudgingly praised because he breaks with Kant's contempt for animals. But Regan, and Singer also, still have a rationalist taint. Each in his own way proceeds from a purely abstract basis of respect for the needs of others:

> Unfortunately, contemporary animal rights theorists, in their reliance on theory that derives from the mechanistic premises of Enlightenment epistemology (natural rights in the case of Regan and utilitarian calculation in the case of Singer) and in their suppression/denial of emotional knowledge, continue to employ Cartesian, or objectivist, modes even while they condemn the scientific practices enabled by them.[6]

But the project of an ethics based on compassion and sympathy is deeply flawed. Compassion and sympathy are entirely concrete. How, then, is one to balance sympathy for a victim with sympathy for the perpetrator? This is the kind of question posed when a suburban gardener wishes (humanely) to expel a woodchuck from his flower bed. To decide which one of them is more worthy of compassion requires an abstract basis of comparison. Perhaps we could dispense with *legislating* rules and simply work from case to case. But evaluations change with changing sensibilities, and unless each caring choice we make sets some sort of precedent for like situations in the future, the outcome has to be chaotic. If we start each time *de novo*, our decisions will depend only on our psychic makeup and perhaps our passing fancy. One could never evaluate or predict the decisions of a court of law in which everything—the determination of "guilt" or "innocence" and the sentence, if any—depends completely on the personality of the judge and how he or she feels after sympathetic reaction to each case taken by itself. Indeed, the very notion of a case begins to dissolve when there is no law in terms of which the issue can be framed.

Difficulties of this sort can be illustrated by reflection on Carol Gilligan's now famous hypothetical case of Heinz and the druggist. Heinz cannot pay for medicine desperately needed by his wife because the drugstore price is beyond his means and the druggist is unyielding. Jake, a boy of eleven, rather quickly justifies theft of the drugs as a solution. Jake's female counterpart, Amy, would eschew theft and instead suggest further discussion with the druggist, renewed attempts to borrow money, or discussions between Heinz and his wife as to how they might raise the money for the payment in some other way. Gilligan, adding further evidence and more data, concludes that this is typical of the difference in moral psychology between men and women. The male appeals to a higher law, to a more ultimate principle that overrides the right of property in order to save a life. The female appeals to the ultimate connectedness of each of us with all:

> Both children thus recognize the need for agreement but see it as mediated in different ways—he impersonally through systems of logic and law, she personally through communication in relationship.[7]

Gilligan carefully abstains from valuing one point of view over the other. But she wishes to do justice (as it were) to the ethic of care which has been so persistently overlooked in male-dominated societies and male-dominated theorizing about morality. The voice of equal justice should have its place. "Yet in the different voice of women lies the truth of an ethic of care, the tie between relationship and responsibility, and the origins of aggression in the failure of connection" (173). Gilligan speaks of these as "two different modes." Both are part of the larger human experience but they are "truths . . . carried by different modes of language and thought" (174).

I believe that, even in this modest form, an ethic of care is ultimately untenable. Sooner or later, as Gilligan herself points out, a decision must be reached. Heinz's dilemma must ultimately be resolved one way or another. Although the young Amy was unable fully to face the problem of "what if . . . "(29), more mature women reluctantly conclude that Heinz might finally be forced to steal (114). This conclusion, we might add, is potentially and implicitly reducible to rules: if Heinz's wife is on the point of death and cannot wait; if friends and neighbors have refused to lend the necessary funds; if Heinz has pleaded with the druggist for mercy and the latter has remained adamant; if Heinz is willing to reimburse the druggist as soon as possible. In such circumstances, roughly approximated, even the ethic of care would presumably countenance a theft.

Let us note, furthermore, that justice itself, following from the rationalist ethics of equality and rights, points to pretty much the same analysis. A court of law would presumably suspend Heinz's sentence, or might even find him innocent, if he had responded properly to some or all of the above questions. And a moral philosopher, indeed even a Kantian moral philosopher, would find that what Heinz had done was right.

Donovan might protest at this point that the choices put to Jake and Amy arise only because our institutions force them upon us. The problem is neither Heinz nor the druggist but the political system. As now constituted, the institutions even of a democracy are unfair to the poor because they do not guarantee an adequate level of medical care and pharmaceutical resources. What seems to be a purely ethical problem thus merges with the issue of political reform.[8]

Let us suppose, however, that Heinz lives in the best possible democratic welfare state. He asks and receives a prescription from a doctor on which the survival of his wife depends, but a bureaucrat has failed to transmit it. Heinz is still confronted with a dilemma. Should he break into the bureaucrat's office or force the druggist to give him the medicine without a prescription? The kind of moral problem posed by Gilligan thus reappears, and will not be banished in any real world set of institutions, no matter how desirable they may be.

The moral imperative thus does not depend on the ethic of care as an independent consideration. The druggist in Gilligan's example is required to respect Heinz's wife as an end and not to treat her only as a means to make a profit. Statutory law, which follows from an implicit social contract based on the moral imperative, does not regard the right of property as an absolute and pays attention, through all sorts of subsidiary regulations, to the circumstances of its use. The ethics of care, on the other hand, cannot be similarly encompassing. It has to take the starting point of its ethical considerations from outside itself. In the Heinz dilemma, this starting point is the basic right of private property. Gilligan does not postulate full communism, which a pure ethics of care might justify. Rather she presupposes the law of private property as a given. Hence while the moral imperative is autonomous, the ethic of care is not. The former must, accordingly, be primary.[9]

The weakness of the ethic of care without a framework from outside also applies to respect for animals. Its proponents strongly recommend concern for individuals of other species. But without the moral imperative, the ethic of care all too easily collapses into welfareism. It has to pick up grounds from somewhere, and the "reasons" that it finds, as Francione argues, are all too often imported uncritically from existing cultural norms. Thus animals are still treated as if they were property. By implication they appear as things which can be owned. But they are to be treated "humanely."

This criticism does not apply to all feminists. Josephine Donovan, for example, calls for a "feminist reconstruction of the world" that includes almost everything demanded by an uncompromising theory of rights.[10] It is hard to understand, therefore, why she criticizes Regan on rights for his "absolutist stance."

This inconsistency about Regan's stance, I believe, points to the underlying problem. Without a critical theory of rights, the ecofeminist position lacks definite moorings. On that account, the ecofeminist is all too likely to slide into welfareism which, however laudable, does not give animals their due. To this extent, Francione's condemnation of the position is justified:

> Rights theory requires the *abolition* of the institutionalized exploitation of animals. Ecofeminism assumes the legitimacy of institutionalized exploitation as part of the normative context in which the ethic of care is to be applied. I concede that the rules often provide only indeterminate normative guidance and that other values (including the ethics of care) may be useful or necessary to decide particular situations. But the ethic of care is relevant to deciding whether we should eat *this particular animal* or use *this particular animal* in an experiment only if the institutional exploitation of animals in science is accepted as a general matter.[11]

This is not to hold that care in the sense of compassion is not a powerful resource in the movement for animal rights. The law is often hard, and with respect to animals notoriously so. It often needs reforming, and the quest for reform is almost always awakened by compassion. But compassion can also be erratic and destructive unless it is guided by rational considerations. The ultimate criterion for reform must therefore be the moral imperative.

The case for an ethics of care, finally, is unjust not only to reasoning generally but to Kant in particular. In his *Metaphysics of Morals*, the first section of the first chapter of part II is entitled "On the Duty of Love to Other Human Beings." Throughout his work on ethics, and here too as well, Kant warns against love, compassion, or respect for others as the ground or motive of action. Such feelings, though, are not only appropriate but owed when they accompany rationally motivated acts of duty owed to others:

> *Love* and *respect* are the feelings that accompany the carrying out of these duties. They can be considered separately (each by itself) and can also exist separately (one can *love* one's neighbor though he might deserve but little *respect*, and can show him the respect necessary for every human being regardless of the fact that he would hardly be judged worthy of love). But they are basically always united by the [moral] law into one duty. . . . So we shall acknowledge that we are under obligation to help someone poor; but since the favor we do implies that his well-being depends on our generosity, and this humbles him, it is our duty to behave as if our help is merely what is due him or but a slight service of love, and to spare him humiliation and maintain his respect for himself.[12]

Thus Kant can be justly faulted for failing to include animals as moral patients, but not for disregarding feeling. Feeling and sentiment are ruled out only as the ultimate ground of morals generally.

Regan too—whose idea of rights is often dismissed as too abstract—is also targeted unfairly by the ecofeminists. In his *The Thee Generation* Regan looks forward to a coming generation of service: of giving, not taking, of commitment to principles not material possessions, of communal compassion not conspicuous consumption. If the defining question of the present generation is What can I get for me? the central question of this new generation is What can I do for thee?[13]

What, then, are the possibilities in religion? I believe that there does not now exist in any major religion a fully satisfactory alternative to a theory of animal rights based squarely on the moral imperative of reason. This applies even if the scientific and cosmological difficulties are bracketed. Although Judaism, Christianity, and Islam all look forward to a transcendental community in which some, many, or all humans will be reconciled to God and to each other, these faiths have traditionally resisted the idea of salvation for other sentient species. This restriction, no doubt, is sometimes contested. In Judaism animals may be included in the age to come. In Christianity there is a minority position that embraces the resurrection and redemption not only of all humans, but of all (higher) animals as well. Such expectations, which go back at least to Isaiah, have been vigorously restated for modern Judaism by Abraham Kook.[14] In Christianity the idea of animal resurrection appears at least as early as Irenaeus[15] and is powerfully developed in our time by Andrew Linzey[16] and Stephen Webb,[17] among others. Most, although not all, theologians of this persuasion are also proponents of animal rights as well. In Islam also there are strong indications of animal resurrection although that seems not to have been developed by Muslim theologians into a theory of animal rights.[18]

In any case, the theological mainstream in Judaism and Christianity also stops short of full acknowledgment of animal rights. Judaism, to be sure, has a noble tradition of concern for the welfare of animals. In the book of Genesis, God would have not only humans but even animals be vegetarians; and vegetarianism, after all, is one major aspect of full commitment to animal rights. But in Genesis 9:2–4 God grants Noah and all humanity express and permanent permission to eat meat. In the Hebrew Bible animal sacrifice is also required, and orthodox Jews still accept it in principle although avoiding the practice on one pretext or another. Christianity has given up animal sacrifice. But the synoptic Gospels portray Jesus as eating fish and do not rule out his eating meat. The practice of animal sacrifice as well as the consumption of meat continues in Islam.

These positions are rooted in the Bible and the Qur'an, and despite all the efforts on the part of animal rights theologians, I do not see how these limitations on animal rights could be fully removed from any of the monotheistic religions without direct alteration or excision of essential sections of the sacred texts. Some attempts have been made, especially among Christians.[19] But they have not had anything like wide acceptance, and this is not the place for comment on the exegetical and textual issues.[20]

At first sight, the great religio-metaphysical systems of the East seem to offer a workable alternative because they are fully committed, at least in principle, to respect for animals. Most often they require their adherents, and especially their elite or their monks, to practice universal compassion toward all sentient beings as a condition for achieving nirvana. But here too compassion is subject to caprice and extremism. The goal of these religions, nirvana, is the final extinction of the self. But the self must first go through a cycle of reincarnation from lower to higher existences, and descent in the scale of being is also possible. Animals, therefore, as well as humans, can commit sins for which they are punished in a future incarnation. Hence the bizarre stories of heroic and ideal self-sacrifice by humans for the sake of an animal. Such, for example, is the Buddhist legend of the prince who allows himself to be eaten by a hungry tigress lest she commit the sin of devouring her cubs.[21] The rationalist perspective rules out such extremism. Animals cannot commit a sin because they do not act by recognition of a law.

6

Conflict of Rights
and Environmentalism

Conflict between animals and humans over the use of
nature is likely to continue endlessly. Where this
struggle is not self-limited by humans, the animals
invariably lose—with tragic results both for species
and for their individual members. There are certain
tragedies, of course, that presumably cannot be
avoided. A species may become extinct for reasons
beyond human control. Individual animals may be
killed or starve to death. Hunting by tribal peoples is
likely to continue. But the displacement of animals
for agriculture and other human enterprises poses an
ethical problem. Both humans and animals have a
right to nature, and each has that right independent
of the other. In the absence of competition, each
species pursues its own well-being. But conflicts
inevitably arise between animals and humans which,
although ordinarily settled by mere force, ought to be
adjudicated in the light of reason. The issue of environmental use, moreover, is especially interesting
since answers here apply generally to any conflict of
right between animals and humans.

Suppose a piece of land on which a man is growing
vegetables, and suppose also that his acquisition of
that land was originally legitimate. We are likely to
agree that the landholder is entitled to drive off deer

or other animals, by force if need be, if they enter upon his land and do damage to his crop. He would be acting by a right of self-defense, which belongs to every creature when its life or means of living is attacked. This much seems uncontroversial.

But now let us suppose that this same farmer lives on a frontier and needs to expand his activities to unused land—not to hunt game or to trap for furs, but simply to cultivate land that has never been used before by humans. Some animals will inevitably be driven out, and some of these are likely to die as a result. It might thus seem, on first thought, that these animals have been deprived of a right of use which is theirs by the rule of prior possession.

Yet on further reflection, we can see that the distribution of right between human and animal had not as yet been settled. The use of land is not assigned by nature in advance to one species or another. As between any two or more species nature belongs to no one; it is *res nullius*. When we read of the genesis of property rights in classical political thought, the authors have tacitly assumed that the entirety of nature belongs to the human species. Their only problem, then, is how nature's resources may be equitably divided among humans. Animals, either as individuals or as species, do not participate in any such agreement either with each other or with humans. As between animals and humans there are merely two fundamental claims in competition with each other.

In this conflict, I would argue, there is a rebuttable presumption in favor of the human claim. I do not hold that the quality of human life is better than an animal's, nor do I think that a human life is preferable, all things being equal, because it affords more opportunities for satisfaction. It appears rather that human beings have some obligation to favor the claim of their own species. This is not the same as to presume that human individuals are always to be favored in any conflict of right with animals. The decision will always depend on the interest of the human species as a whole.

At first thought, this viewpoint may seem to contradict everything that I have said so far. I have emphatically insisted that no human interest, collective or individual, can ever justify the exploitation of individuals belonging to another species. But not every removal of animals from a newly entered zone of human activity is a case of exploitation. The question need not be posed as the use of animals for human purposes and interests.

The issue, as I wish to frame it here, is whether the intended expansion of human activity will enhance or diminish the quality of human life, quite apart from the exploitation of animals as means. One major consideration in making that determination must be the impact on the life of animals and the quality of the environment in general. Respect for the integrity of nature and opposition to mere expansion of human numbers for its own sake are thus built in to the criterion. In this sense limited displacement of animals, humanely conducted, can be legitimate even though the cost to animals is great.

For Tom Regan, the theory of animal rights points to a very different outcome on the environmental issue. I shall try to show later on in this chapter that many of his reflections in this area are mistaken. But on the larger theoretical question I believe his insight is indispensable. Regan's general reflections on how conflicts of interest between animals and humans ought to be resolved are not only correct but very powerful; and I shall argue that, properly pursued, they support the view that I have outlined above. In other words, they serve to justify a qualified priority for humans in the environment as well as in other areas.

Regan's basic qualification on animal rights follows from the reflections that death is a greater loss to humans than to animals because a human life offers more possibilities of satisfaction. Hence in certain exceptional circumstances of conflict, which he calls "prevention cases," the interest of human life should properly prevail. He supposes a situation in which a mixed group of animals and humans face inevitable death if nothing is done, but in which some individuals can be rescued if the rest are abandoned or sacrificed. His illustration of this principle is the "lifeboat case" which is well known in the literature on animal rights.[1]

Regan imagines an overloaded lifeboat that is about to sink. The occupants include four humans and a dog, all of roughly equal weight. All five will drown if nothing is done. But four of them can be saved if one of them is thrown overboard. Which, then, Regan asks, is the morally right decision? Should the four humans cast lots (adding one lot for the dog), or should they simply throw the dog overboard?[2] In other words, which is it to be, the dog or one of the humans?

Ordinary prereflective intuition, at least for most people, points to the sacrifice of the dog. Surprisingly enough, Regan, who holds that all mammals of a year or more in age have equal inherent value, agrees. In an emergency, where one must go if all are not to die, he believes that some choice must be made. He thus excludes the option of allowing all to drown. If one of the five must thus be thrown overboard, then the dog is the appropriate victim because each human, Regan argues, has more to lose from the termination of his or her life than does the dog. A human life ordinarily has more opportunities for satisfaction than a dog's. All things being equal, therefore, a human life must be preferred in a "prevention case." Yet both are still said to have equal inherent value. "All on board," writes Regan,

> have equal inherent value and an equal prima facie right not to be harmed. Now, the harm that death is, is a function of the opportunities for satisfaction it forecloses, and no reasonable person would deny that the death of any of the four humans would be a greater prima facie loss, and thus a greater prima facie harm, than would be true in the case of the dog. Death for the dog, in short, though a harm, is not comparable to the harm that death would be for any of the humans. (324)

Some commentators on Regan have characterized this comparison as a glaring contradiction in his overall position. This is the view especially of utilitarian critics like Peter Singer and Dale Jamieson. Others, like Steve Sapontzis and Evelyn Pluhar, are more sympathetic but find his argument too crude. And even a sympathetic commentator like Gary L. Francione is unhappy with some of the consequences to which it leads. I shall in what follows evaluate these criticisms of Regan on the lifeboat case and then offer some suggestions of my own.[3]

The fullest and most uncompromising criticism is from Peter Singer. "I confess to some difficulty," Singer says,

> in understanding the reasoning here. If Regan's position were based on the principle of equal consideration of interests, he would be able to argue that the people have a greater interest in living than the dog, either because of the greater benefit that continued life will be to them, or because they, but not the dog, have plans, hopes, and desires for the future which will be thwarted if they do not continue to live. But Regan seeks to base his position on a principle of equal inherent value. How can he do this while still allowing us to add up the opportunities for satisfaction a life contains, and on the basis of this addition, judge a normal human life to be more valuable than a normal canine life? How can this be reconciled with the notion of equal inherent value as something distinct from the value of the experiences or satisfactions a being may have?[4]

Singer does not question Regan's idea of benefits in the lifeboat case. As a utilitarian, he does not doubt that the satisfactions that individuals might feel can be compared in broadly quantitative terms, and he readily agrees that the humans in the lifeboat case ought to have priority. His essential criticism is what he finds to be a fundamental inconsistency in Regan's overall position. His comparison of satisfactions in the lifeboat case, holds Singer, implies a utilitarian calculus. Yet he rightly notes that the very point of Regan's principle of inherent value was to rule out utilitarianism as a guide to moral choice and to replace it with a theory of rights. Singer, as a utilitarian, would restore consistency by having Regan abandon the theory of rights; and this is substantially Jamieson's conclusion as well.[5]

There is a misunderstanding on Singer's part, however, which has to do, I believe, with the meaning of inherent value. Regan does not fully ground that concept as he states it. We have seen, however, that it follows from a reflective moral intuition that mammals may not be used merely as means to human ends. This is his meaning when he speaks of "equal inherent value" in all mammals of one year or more in age. But the phrase is perhaps unfortunate semantically. It can easily be taken to mean that there is some equal *quantity* of value in each such sentient being; that can be seriously misleading, suggesting some equal potential for pleasure or pain. Equal inherent value means only that every mammal and, indeed, every sentient being has an equal claim not to be treated merely as an instrument. All sentient beings are thereby *morally* equal. Inherent value is not something that can be measured empirically. It follows directly from Regan's basic intuition.

I do not see that instrumentalization occurs in Regan's version of the lifeboat case. Clearly, either the dog or one of the men must be sacrificed to save the others, and whoever is chosen for that sacrifice will serve as a means to the others' well-being. But the sinking lifeboat did not arise from anyone's deliberate act. The choice of sacrificing one individual is imposed upon the occupants lest *all* on board should die. Only in that sense is the act deliberate.

Such rescue situations, or "prevention cases," come in many forms, and in all of them an exception must be made to the rule against knowingly harming to the innocent. Yet the rule against turning sentient and conscious beings into instruments remains intact. That the normal rights of some must be overridden if all are not to suffer is not a situation that the rescuer has deliberately brought about.

Respect for inherent value, furthermore, also determines our choice of whom we should favor in a prevention situation. Regan, even here, concedes nothing to utilitarianism for he avoids aggregating benefits and harms. His rule for prevention cases is to determine the magnitude of loss that each individual would suffer and to give priority to those who face the greatest harm. Where harms must be compared, it may well be that like injuries will not lead to like effects: death to a dog may be a lesser harm than death to a human. But this, despite appearances, does not violate the rule of equal respect for the inherent value of each individual. If we did not compare harms it would be possible for an individual whose loss was less to have priority, which would violate the equal consideration required by the very recognition of inherent value. In this instance, equal consideration requires recognizing differences in threatened loss.

Regan offers two basic cases of prevention in order to illustrate his principle. In the first, he hypothesizes a mine disaster in which fifty-one survivors are trapped below ground. All of them will die unless they are rescued promptly. But there are two mine shafts; in one of them there are fifty survivors, and in the other only one. Furthermore, survivors cannot be removed from either shaft without blowing up the other. The harm done to each miner by death, finally, would be roughly the same.

A utilitarian would simply add up the utilities and opt without hesitation for the fifty. Regan, however, would arrive at the same conclusion by a different route. Since the loss to each individual by death is roughly the same, equal respect for each requires us to take numbers into account. To override the right of the many would be to override an equal right fifty times rather than once. Individuals among the fifty would thus be subject to discrimination. Where, then, the harms to be suffered are comparable as here, moral choice in a prevention case is governed by what Regan calls the miniride principle:

> Special considerations aside, when we must choose between overriding the rights of the many who are innocent or the rights of the few who are innocent, and when each affected individual will be harmed in a prima facie comparable way, then we ought to choose to override the rights of the few in preference to overriding the rights of the many.[6]

Although the conceptual differences are clear, the results of the miniride procedure are very similar to aggregation. In Regan's second illustration, however, the harms suffered are not equal; here the differences between his approach and utilitarian aggregation are immediately evident. In this second example, all would be harmed but some few would fare worse than the others. If all individuals are to be treated with equal respect, it is the many who would suffer less who must undergo harm if a choice is unavoidable. We are morally obliged by what Regan calls the "worse-off" principle to rescue the worse-off individuals without regard to numbers. Thus in the lifeboat example, the humans face the greater harm, and since the inherent value of the humans and the dog must be respected equally, the worse-off principle requires us to choose in favor of the humans. Were we to override the right of any of the humans, the dog, who would suffer the lesser harm, would be accorded undue value.

In this situation, as has been said, numbers do not count. The individual who would be worse off retains priority over all the others. "The lifeboat case," notes Regan,

> would not be *morally* any different if we supposed that the choice had to be made, not between a single dog and the four humans, but between these humans and any number of dogs. Let the number of dogs be as large as one likes; suppose they number a million; and suppose the lifeboat will support only four survivors. Then the rights view still implies that, special considerations apart, the million dogs should be thrown overboard and the four humans saved. (324–325)

Singer objects that in this second case, which he rightly takes to be decisive, Regan is simply being stubborn in refusing to allow aggregation. "Suppose we had to choose," he asks,

> between sacrificing a chimpanzee and a dog. Presumably Regan would allow us to argue, in the same manner that he has argued in the case of the human beings and the dog, that the life of the chimpanzee has greater opportunities for satisfaction, and hence it is the dog who should be sacrificed. Does it still follow that we should sacrifice a million dogs for one chimpanzee? Would the same point hold if it were a rhesus monkey rather than a chimpanzee? If so, is this not merely a stubborn refusal to allow numbers to count? If not, if numbers are allowed to count when we compare different non-human animals, why shouldn't they count in cases involving human ones as well? Was Regan's example perhaps trading on our (speciesist) intuition that *no* amount of canine satisfaction can add up to *any* amount of human satisfaction?[7]

In a brief exchange with Singer,[8] Regan does not take up this objection. But he might have replied that the gap between human and animal possibilities is very much larger than that between two species of non-human mammals. The difference in possible satisfactions between the life of a dog and that of a chimpanzee is presumably small. But where differences are relatively small, Regan might be justified in saying that chimpanzees and dogs, caught on an overloaded lifeboat, would be facing comparable harm.[9] Here, then, numbers would have to count, although not in the sense of aggregating utilities, but merely to insure that all are treated equally. The choice of which individuals to save would thus be covered by the rule that Regan applies to the mine disaster case and which he calls the miniride procedure.

My conclusion, then, is that Regan's utilitarian critics do not do justice to the way in which he applies the concept of inherent value to prevention cases. The point is nicely illustrated in this comment by Peter Singer:

> Even if Regan can show that his views about the lifeboat case are consistent with his principle of equal inherent value, he must still face an even more difficult task: to explain the discrepancy between his readiness to throw a million dogs out of a lifeboat in order to save one human being, and his refusal to allow even one dog to be used in a lethal—but painless—experiment to save one or more human beings. Regan is aware of the apparent inconsistency, and quite explicitly states that his rights-based theory does not allow the experiment. His explanation of the difference between killing the dog as an experiment and killing it by throwing it out of the lifeboat, is that when we perform such experiments we treat animals "as if their value were reducible *merely* to their possible utility relative to human interests. . . . " But why should this be so? Why should we not say, as Regan said in the lifeboat case, that we must choose between the deaths of the people or the dog, and although we recognize that death is harmful to the dog, it is a lesser harm for the dog than it would be for the people?[10]

Singer here passes over a point that is fundamental to Regan's whole position. In Regan's theory the lethal experiment and the lifeboat case are radically different situations. In the first, the dog is deliberately taken as an instrument for human purposes, violating the principle that the inherent value of all individuals is to be respected equally. In the lifeboat case the choice is unavoidably imposed. Here respect for inherent value dictates that we choose for salvation those who face the greater harm. The sacrifice in prevention cases of the one less harmed thus cannot be generalized. The rule of the lifeboat case, in other words, is not the normal rule. As Regan says more than once in *The Case for Animal Rights*, it is a clearly defined exception to the rule against the use of animals as instruments. "What the rights view implies should be done in *exceptional* cases—and prevention cases, including lifeboat cases, *are* exceptional cases—cannot be fairly generalized to unexceptional cases" (325).

In his subsequent exchange with Singer, Regan repeats the grounds of this distinction and spells it out in some detail by way of a reply to this particular objection. But even now Singer seems less than fully responsive to the issue. In his reply to Regan's reply he seems inadvertently to concede the entire point:

> He [Regan] now responds that the lifeboat case is different from animal experimentation, because the animals in the lifeboat have not been coerced into the situation in which they are at risk of harm. This difference, however, does not distinguish the lifeboat situation from all possible circumstances in which animals might be experimented upon.
>
> Suppose, for instance, that a new and fatal virus affects both dogs and humans. Scientists believe that the only way to save the lives of any of those affected is to carry out experiments on some of them. The subjects of the experiment will die, but the knowledge gained will mean that others affected by the disease will live. In this situation the dogs and the humans are in equal peril and the peril is not the result of coercion. If Regan thinks a dog should be thrown out of a lifeboat so that the humans in it can be saved, he cannot consistently deny that we should experiment on a diseased dog to save diseased humans.[11]

Singer has constructed a situation in which Regan, consistent with his principles, would indeed have to retreat from "complete abolition of the harmful use of animals in science.'"[12] But in the construction of the case as Singer stipulates it, the experiment would be permitted only on the utterly bizarre condition that the entire population of dogs and humans faces certain death from a plague which can surely be stopped by the conduct of "experiments" that are only now to be conducted. But this is simply to replicate a prevention case in "science" which has all the characteristics of Regan's lifeboat situation. Given these conditions, Regan could readily agree to experiments on animals without any retreat from his basic position on inherent value. On the other hand, the use of experiments in Singer's example could not be generalized to any of the usual contemporary practices. Hence Singer is still unable to show any inconsistency in Regan's fundamental argument. He has "won" his point about lethal experiments on animals only by implicitly accepting the distinction between lifeboat cases and all others.

Still other critics accept Regan's idea of inherent value but hold that he has used it illegitimately in his solution of the lifeboat problem. Francione is more egalitarian than Regan, and he is troubled by a solution to the lifeboat problem so profoundly unfavorable to animals. For it implies that in any contest between human and animal interests, the animals are bound to lose.[13] Regan's error, he maintains, is his program of comparing harms, which he, as well as other commentators, believes is oversimplified. Thus, Sapontzis, whom Francione quotes approvingly, categorically denies that we have any right to believe (as Regan does) that the life of humans offers more opportunities for greater satisfaction than the lives of animals. We cannot know, and so "cannot enjoy the life of a dog, a bird, a bat, or a dolphin. Consequently, we cannot appreciate the subtleties of smell, sight, sound, and touch that these animals can apparently appreciate." (219) The satisfactions of animals, furthermore, although fewer than ours, may perhaps be more intense. In any event the quality and strength of experiences will depend on the character of the individual who feels it and not on our imagination of it. "A life that looks as if it would be a hard and dull one for us to lead (e.g., the life of a beaver) may be experienced by the one who lives it to be enjoyable and fulfilling" (220).

Sapontzis concludes that we have no way of comparing the utility of lives as between animals and humans:

> It follows that if we consider the lives of a dog and a human, for example, which are very different lives but which, let us presume, are both experienced by those living them as enjoyable and fulfilling, it is impossible to determine which life has the greater utilitarian value. The human life may have greater variety to it, and the human might feel frustrated if she or he were given the dog's life to lead. But that is irrelevant to the question of whether its life is more or less enjoyable and fulfilling for the dog than the human life is enjoyable and fulfilling for the human. Since we cannot feel what the animal feels, we cannot determine whether a human gets more or less enjoyment and fulfillment from his enjoyable and fulfilling life than an animal gets from its enjoyable and fulfilling life. (221)

Even more far-reaching is Thomas Nagel's skeptical reflection in his essay, "What Is It Like To Be a Bat?" "My imagination," says Nagel, "tells me what it is like for *me* to behave like a bat. But that is not the question. I want to know what it is like for a *bat* to be a bat."[14]

Nagel's view, which seems to rule out any comparison whatever, is perhaps too sweeping. We do have some idea, however imperfect, of what other beings' feelings could be like.[15] As Sapontzis puts it, "Even if we cannot directly experience the pleasures of other life forms, we can, if we will make the effort to observe animals closely, come to understand which ways of life provide them more enjoyment and fulfillment"(109). Indeed, to deny all credit to our constructions about other minds points a path to destructive skepticism. For just as we cannot fully know what it means to "be" a bat, so we cannot fully know what it means to "be" another person.

Sapontzis's warning that we cannot be sure about the intensity and special overtones of feelings when we compare animal and human lives is thus the stronger objection. And in this he is seconded by Pluhar.

Our canine B might be considerably less intelligent than [our human] A, but his joie de vivre does not appear to be any less! The comparative richness of A's and B's experiences and interests is simply not relevant in this context: the degree of harm suffered [by death] is a function of how much what has been snatched away means to *them*. . . . If A and B both value living and are in the prime of life, they would be harmed equally by death, no matter how "dull" B is in comparison to A.[16]

But Pluhar also believes that Regan's solution to the lifeboat problem requires even more than the ability to compare the lives of individuals in the abstract. The life of a particular individual in a given species will vary with its circumstances. The possibilities of future expectations in a healthy youngster are greater than those of a sickly octogenarian. Suppose, furthermore, that the youngster is a dog and the oldster is a human. Pluhar's objection applies across species lines as well as within.

I believe that both of these objections can be overcome. The comparison to which Sapontzis objects can be carried out, at least very roughly. In his *Practical Ethics* Peter Singer suggests—very cautiously and tentatively—that at least some comparisons are possible. He supposes that a human being can assume or come close to achieving a neutral "third" consciousness between, let us say, a horse and a human, and then, from the standpoint of that third consciousness, make a choice between the two lives. The horse and the human are assumed to be as happy as any individual of that species can reasonably expect to be. The human then turns himself first into the horse and then into the human, experiencing the lives of both. In a third and relatively neutral state of consciousness the human would remember the two lives it experienced and "would then be deciding, in effect, between the value of the life of a horse (to the horse) and the value of the life of a human (to the human).[17]

Once the superiority of human lives in general is recognized, a reply to Pluhar's objection is also available. Where many human lives are at stake in an emergency we are expected to make choices about which to save that do not normally depend on comparison of life expectancies. They are expectations rather than binding rules and need not be morally binding. But they are loosely rooted in instinct, in the slow growth of tacit agreement, or in both elements acting together. Such conventions, however explained, do not contradict what we have said about the equality of inherent value in all sentient creatures. Our conventionally founded duty to aid this human rather than that one does not mean that we may treat any individual, human or animal, as a mere means to human advantage in any ordinary set of circumstances.

In emergency situations involving a choice between animals and humans, I must follow the rule of comparative inherent value. But where the choice is between two humans with different claims, such as those imagined by Pluhar, I am bound to follow established conventions. Rules of emergency, like women and children first on a sinking ship, seem to have become widely accepted. The principle may be different in different times and cultures. But there will always be some rule that determines which choice will be considered proper. The rule for ordinary circumstances, like boarding a bus, is of course that everyone is equal—the rich and the poor, the scientist and the layman. But triage may be justified in certain kinds of emergencies.

I believe that these considerations also apply to the choice between saving a young dog and saving an aged human. The conventionally based duties owed to members of our own species seem to have some carryover to species of mammals close to ours. I personally love dogs. But faced with harsh necessity, like that encountered in the lifeboat, I would sacrifice a dog before I would destroy a primate. Would I sacrifice a million dogs to save one primate? I don't know. But neither do I know whether I would sacrifice a million males to save one woman!

Francione, referring to Regan's position, worries lest the principles of the lifeboat case mean that all conflicts of interest between animals and humans will be decided in favor of the latter. Francione is sympathetic to Regan's concept of inherent value, although he prefers to say that animals cannot be made into the property of humans. He is also perfectly clear as to Regan's distinction between routine subordination of animal to human interests and the subordination of animal interests in prevention cases.[18] He also believes that the characteristics of prevention cases are clearly and unobjectionably defined. Francione is thus satisfied that Regan has fully demonstrated that animals have rights and cannot be treated as mere property. But he disagrees with Regan's judgment in favor of the humans where the otherwise legitimate rights of animals and humans come into conflict. He contends that the judgment not only requires a quantitative comparison of harms, but that it is an implicit lapse into "perfectionism"—into the idea, in other words, that the human capacity for satisfactions is not only greater but better. "Although Regan," Francione comments,

> may be correct to argue that his resolution of the lifeboat example does not appeal explicitly to perfectionism as advocating the *routine* subordination of rightholders, his resolution does appeal to a supposed human "excellence" (the ability to pursue opportunities for satisfaction). But to say that this virtue may be appealed to only in exceptional cases is nevertheless to say that *in that class of cases*, there is routine subordination based on a supposed virtue possessed by one *class* of rightholders.[19]

Among friends of animals, the accusation of perfectionism is a serious charge. We have already seen that this is an approach to valuation that Regan, no less than Francione, vehemently rejects. According to the perfectionist idea of justice as it appears in Aristotle and Nietzsche among others, "what individuals are due, as a matter of justice, depends on the degree to which they possess a certain cluster of virtues or excellences, including intellectual and artistic talents and a character that expresses itself in performance of heroic or magnificent deeds."[20] Regan is unwilling to accept perfectionism in any form:

> Perfectionist theories of justice are morally pernicious, providing, as they do, the foundation of the most objectionable forms of social,

political, and legal discrimination—chattel slavery, rigid caste systems, and gross disparities in the quality of life available to citizens in the same state, for example. But perfectionist theories are objectionable at a deeper level. Whether individuals have the talent necessary to acquire the favored virtues (e.g., ability to do higher mathematics) is beyond their control. . . . Those who are born with intellectual or artistic gifts have not done anything to deserve preferred treatment. (234)

This characterization of perfectionism, widespread in the literature of animal rights, is one with which Francione basically agrees. But in my opinion Francione's judgment of Regan is too hasty. Aristotle's perfectionism is no doubt based on an unacceptable idea of hierarchy in nature; Nietzsche's doctrine is less a doctrine of morality than a critique of moral law as such. But Regan, for better or worse, adheres to a strictly quantitative comparison of harms, which is not perfectionist in principle, and may, as I have suggested, be qualified by convention.

In any event, Francione believes that the consequences of the lifeboat argument are more unfortunate for animals than might appear from Regan's exposition. The worse-off principle, he argues, cannot be confined to prevention cases involving dramatic choices of life and death. The exceptions to equal treatment of animals would have to extend to every conflict between animal and human interests:

The problem is that in light of Regan's analysis of the lifeboat example, it would seem that he is committed to resolving virtually *every* human/animal conflict in favor of the human. This does not, as some have suggested, mean that he is on a slippery slope back to vivisection. On the contrary, Regan can claim that the respect principle is always violated in cases of institutionalized exploitation. But it does give nonhumans a somewhat pyrrhic victory. Animals may no longer be regarded as property, but their interests will nevertheless not prevail most of the time. (87)

Francione thus concludes that Regan's theory of animal rights works only for the ordinary cases of institutional subordination, such as the general use of animals for food. But he believes that Regan should, and presumably could, have stopped at that, and holds that "it was wholly unnecessary for Regan even to discuss the lifeboat example." He thinks that at the present time we do not have, and must still develop, an effective approach to conflicts of rights between humans and animals. Regan's efforts, accordingly, are premature and entail unacceptable results.

I agree with Francione on the results of the lifeboat principle, but I do not go along with his evaluation. The rule that animals may not be used as instruments, treated as mere property, or routinely subordinated to human purposes is no mean gain for animals. On this we would both agree. Among other things, it means that animals may not be eaten, may not be used for human entertainment and amusement, and may not be taken as subjects for biomedical experiments and tests. Where animals have been domesticated, as with pets for example, we are positively obliged to give them nurture and support.

But in all those other cases where there is direct and unavoidable competition between animal and human interests, where one or the other must be sacrificed or both will suffer, animal interests will lose. Here Francione is more or less correct. But in these situations, I suggest that the priority in favor of humans is clearly acceptable. Once the basic rights of animals are recognized, the development and improvement of human society seem to be a higher priority than the maintenance of the animal population. This points to a tragic element in the relationship of humans and animals that seems to be unavoidable on any reasonable account.

Nor can I agree with Francione that the discussion of the lifeboat situation is unnecessary. The basic rights of animals are difficult to affirm without also speaking of their general scope and limits. If the lifeboat situation is an exception to the basic rule of equal treatment, then a consistent rationale must be advanced for choosing humans over animals. But if, as Francione thinks, no such rationale can be given, the basic rule of complete equality must apply universally and without exception. Hence it has to be one way or another. A theory of animal rights that avoids the lifeboat issue would be incomplete and potentially incoherent.

The relevance of the lifeboat case to issues of environmentalism can now be spelled out. Environmentalism often requires a choice between animal and human interests in those uses of nature where one or the other interest must be sacrificed, even though both are otherwise legitimate. Animal rights theorists often become sentimental on this issue, but once the lifeboat case is rightly understood, the lifeboat preference for humans is required as the rule for choice.

Regan too, I believe, abandons the lifeboat principle when he comes to the question of environmentalism. One sentient being, he believes, has as much right of access to nature as another. That limitations on survival are imposed by nature itself he does not deny. Animals are destroyed by many natural causes—but human intervention to preserve the ecology may also cause animals to be destroyed. This outcome, as Regan reflects in *Animal Rights*, is unjustified:

> If, in a prevention situation, we had to choose between saving the last two members of an endangered species or saving another individual who belonged to a species that was plentiful but whose death would be a greater prima facie harm to that individual than the harm that death would be to the two, then the rights view requires that we save that individual. (359)

Noah, the first conservationist, was therefore wrong in saving animals by species. Holism in any form and particularly in the form of the land ethic of Aldo Leopold and his followers is bitterly attacked:

> The difficulties and implications of developing a rights-based environmental ethic . . . should be abundantly clear by now and deserve brief comment before moving on. The difficulties include reconciling the *individualistic* nature of moral rights with the more *holistic* view of nature emphasized by many of the leading environmental thinkers. Aldo Leopold is illustrative of this latter tendency. "A thing is right,"

he states, "when it tends to preserve the integrity, stability, and beauty of the biotic community. It is wrong when it tends otherwise." The implications of this view include the clear prospect that the individual may be sacrificed to the greater biotic good, in the name of "the integrity, stability, and beauty of the biotic community." It is difficult to see how the notion of the rights of the individual could find a home within a view that, emotive connotations to the side, might be fairly dubbed "environmental fascism."[21]

Against Leopold this point is telling, and the proponents of the land ethic have been hard put to defend it. In a frequently cited article written in 1980, J. Baird Callicott, a leading theorist in that tradition, fully recognizes the charge but makes no effort to soften it. Insofar as possible, he counters, we should shake off unhealthy constraints of civilization in our dealings with nature:

There is another approach. Rather than imposing our alienation from nature and natural processes and cycles of life on other animals, we human beings could reaffirm our participation in nature by accepting life as it is given without a sugar coating. Instead of imposing artificial legalities, rights, and so on on nature, we might take the opposite course and accept and affirm natural biological laws, principles, and limitations in the human personal and social spheres. Such appears to have been the posture toward life of tribal people in the past. The chase was relished with its dangers, rigors, and hardships as well as its rewards: animal flesh was respectfully consumed; a tolerance for pain was cultivated; virtue and magnanimity were prized; lithic, floral, and faunal spirits were worshipped; population was routinely optimized by sexual continency, abortion, infanticide, and stylized warfare; and other life forms, although certainly appropriated, were respected as fellow players in a magnificent and awesome, if not altogether idyllic, drama of life.[22]

Although Callicott does not believe that we can return to that pristine condition, he does believe that we can learn from, and be inspired, by it. "The land ethic . . . requires a shrinkage, if at all possible, of the domestic sphere; it rejoices in a recrudescence of wilderness and a renaissance of tribal cultural experience" (57).

Callicott has softened this position in subsequent writings. Some eight years later, in another article often referred to by environmentalists, Callicott is more friendly to the animal rights idea. Having earlier dismissed domesticated animals as denatured artifacts, he has now become deeply impressed by Mary Midgley's idea of a mixed community of domestic life in which humans have a limited but real responsibility for domesticated animals, a responsibility that has been worked out over the ages of human civilization.

Nevertheless, Callicott does not import a fundamental change of doctrine in a way that is consistent with animal rights. Midgley's concept of a mixed community is not, in any event, responsive to a full statement of the rights even of domesticated animals, since it does not recognize their equal inherent rights. The more relevant objection here, however, is that Callicott continues to interpret environmentalism as a mandate to roll back civilization as far as possible:

> Domestic animals are members of the mixed community and ought to enjoy, therefore, all the rights and privileges, whatever they may turn out to be, attendant upon that membership. Wild animals are, by definition, not members of the mixed community . . .
>
> Wild animals, rather, are members of the biotic community. The structure of the biotic community is described by ecology. The duties and obligations of a biotic community ethic or "land ethic," as Leopold called it, may, accordingly, be derived from an ecological description of nature.[23]

This and related passages indicate that the mixed community does not supersede the land ethic but must be integrated as one part of it. If not—that is, if the mixed community and the land ethic simply coexist without an overarching principle—then Callicott's environmental theory is incoherent. In any event, Regan's critique of environmentalism in this form as oppressive remains justified.

In a very recent statement, the threat of incoherence in Callicott seems to materialize. Specifically repudiating the charge of ecofascism in Regan and others, he begins to work out a more complex system of priorities designed to find a compromise between environmental values and human ethics. He strongly protests a rigid interpretation of Leopold's land ethic:

> I never actually endorsed such a position. It is obnoxious and untenable. And I now no longer think that misanthropic prescriptions can be deduced from the Leopold land ethic. . . . I certainly feel that we have duties and obligations to fellow humans (and to humanity as a whole) that supersede the land ethic as I have subsequently explained, although I have by no means abandoned the land ethic.[24]

How, then, are humanist and environmental values to be reconciled? A celebrated solution by Christopher D. Stone is an idea of moral pluralism in which different moral principles are applied ad hoc to different situations and issues. Callicott, correctly in my opinion, rejects moral pluralism as intellectually incoherent and offers an overarching and unifying principle. A reconciliation of the human and the ecological, he thinks, can thus be realized in a hierarchy of principles rather than in, as in Stone, a mere multiplicity thereof. Where we find the primary values to be in conflict, we are to invoke two second-order principles. The first of these second order principles (SOP1) is that obligations arising from membership "in more venerable and intimate communities [e.g., the human family] take precedence over those generated in more recently emerged and impersonal communities [i.e., most of our relationships to plants and animals]." But the second of these second-order principles (SOP2) is the condition under which SOP1 be bypassed. It holds that

> stronger interests (for lack of a better word) generate duties that take precedence over duties generated by weaker interests. For example, while duties to one's own children, all things being equal, properly take precedence over duties to unrelated children in one's municipality,

one would be ethically remiss to shower one's own children with luxuries while unrelated children in one's municipality lacked the bare necessities.[25]

The application of this rule to environmental issues now follows. One can cut down trees for necessary purposes since the interests here are strong. But it is unethical to cut down tall and beautiful trees simply to make a path in the woods, since that cause is light and transient.

Yet this solution, most desirable as a rule of policy, seems to negate environmentalism. SOP1 now gives priority to the needs of the human community. It supposes that humanity as we know it is the outcome of evolutionary processes which have favored the dominance of a species capable of moral community. That mere fact, of course, does not prove that human primacy is right. Even leaving that issue aside, though, Callicott's solution still effectively overrules the land ethic. The primacy of the biotic community taken as a whole, essential to the land ethic, is relinquished. That primacy is now little more than a first look or initial thought. The needs of the biotic community are then subordinated, not the primacy of strong human interests. In either case, humanity and humanity's interests, not the biotic community, have become the ultimate measures of environmental policy.

And this primacy for humans, I believe, is as it should be, and it is compatible with rights for animals because the rule of the lifeboat case applies. The primacy of humans in the environment does not override their moral obligation never to treat any sentient beings as mere instruments. Nevertheless, that rule does *not* apply to conflicts of legitimate interest between animals and humans. In such situations the only obligation is self-restraint *in pursuing the interests of humans*. Regan's sweeping charge in this respect must accordingly be set aside. Very proper and commendable policies based upon the lifeboat principle may well be the kind of thing that he brands as ecological fascism!

There is, after all, an obvious difference between mindless exploitation of nature and intelligent as well as limited use. We thus have every right and also duty to insist on protection of the environment as a basic interest of humanity itself. Indeed, this approach, as we have seen, is latent in Callicott's own most recent statements. What they come to, indeed, is rehabilitation of the old-fashioned idea of conservationism.

Animal rights theorists often object that conservationism is a form of speciesism in which nature exists solely for the pleasure of humanity. It is true that many interventions supported by conservationists do indeed, at least first sight, seem indifferent to the fate of animals and to recognition of their inherent rights. Suppose, for example, that one species of animals is plentiful while another is threatened with extinction, and suppose also that humans here face a "preservation case" in which the numbers of both species cannot coexist in the space available. Conservationist principles would seem to dictate that members of the plentiful species be eliminated. Such a conclusion appears to be indifferent to the rights of the individual animals that are thus to be removed or destroyed.

A very striking illustration of this difficulty is the choice, between deer and "mere" trees faced by sensitive conservationists in Canada. "A growing deer population," writes Angus Taylor,

> had been eating the saplings of the shade-intolerant prized tree species in preference to maple and beech, thus threatening to alter radically the nature of the forest over time. Attempts to capture the deer and move them elsewhere met with little success. When the Ontario Ministry of Natural Resources decided to kill many of the deer in order to protect the fragile forest ecosystem, the plan was opposed, for different reasons, by animal-rights activists, cottagers, aboriginal people, and even hunters.[26]

This choice, made strictly from the standpoint of human interest in conserving the environment, seems at first thought to be a speciesist denial of inherent value in the deer. Yet the decision of the Ontario ministry was unassailable at least in principle. Its interest in the forest was not to saw up the trees for row houses or to make space for a porno theatre. It was to preserve an esthetic and scientific treasure, which, for the reasons we have given, was a legitimate exercise of human primacy. It did not deny the inherent right of the deer not to be used as instruments.

Suppose an imaginary line were to be drawn between that part of the earth's surface inhabited by humans together with their domesticated animals and that part inhabited by animals in the wild. This line is highly imaginary since the wild and the humanized so fully interpenetrate. There are wild beasts in everybody's garden and sometimes in their dwellings also. And there are now parks and other human efforts to maintain environments in what used to be the wilderness. Nevertheless, the imaginary line is useful for analysis of the issues.

At any historical moment the imaginary line may be taken as the frontier in a suspended state of war between humans and wild animals. Both sides have been, and will continue to be, in potential competition for space and resources. No full peace is possible between them since animals cannot make or recognize a treaty. Hence the burden of justice or injustice in the conduct of the war and the duty of delimiting a frontier of truce falls wholly on the human side.

Just conduct of the war by humans means that only as much land and resources are taken from animal use as is necessary for the human species to have a comfortable material and moral life. At least this much seems to follow from the comparison of inherent values in situations of unavoidable conflict. This comparison also implies some right on the part of humans to expand the scope of settlement in order to accommodate a reasonable increase in the number of humans who can be sustained at a comfortable level. All of this, of course, is what is usually regarded as sane and reasonable conservationist policy.

Nevertheless, what often goes unnoticed is that the rights of animals do not disappear on this account. Uses of nature that do not advance the level of human existence are not justified, but rather condemned by this principle of conservation. There is thus a right of animals to unused nature. Unjustified intrusion into their environment is a moral wrong done to the animals affected (as well as to other human beings for whom nature is an important value).

Furthermore, the presumption in favor of humans notwithstanding, this right of animals is a serious restraint. Humans may override this principle only if doing so would enhance their quality of life. Population explosions, wasteful and needless development of housing, the conversion of wilderness into resort areas—all such things are an affront to the higher interests of humans, and precisely for that reason they are also unjust violations of animal interests.

But even when a priority for humans is admitted in the use of nature, it does not in any way curtail the basic rights of animals we have attempted to establish earlier. That animals may not be used as instruments for human purposes is still an absolute. And concern for their inherent value must also apply to procedures for ejecting them when legitimate human interests are threatened. The example of the Ontario Ministry of Natural Resources is again instructive. Humans were entitled to preserve the trees; but the deer were entitled to be removed as humanely as possible, and even at great cost, before extreme measures were employed. Indifference to their treatment would not have been far removed from the attitude that goes with using them as instruments.

If the imaginary line is now erased, and the coexistence of animals and humans in a given area is considered, it is evident that the rights of wild animals within a settled area are even more strictly limited by the priority for human interests. If a human settlement is legitimate to begin with, then the presence of wildlife need be tolerated only if it is not destructive. A gardener in such a settlement need not put up with woodchucks, nor a householder with mice or rats, nor a suburbanite with deer in the backyard. Humans have an overriding right of self-defense in all such situations. The only restriction, once again, is that the removal of the pests be done as humanely as possible. Woodchucks, deer, and even rats are not "pests" as such, but become such in places where humans have a right to be free of them. Yet even so, their unwanted presence is innocent, and they are entitled to humane removal.

Endangered species seem to occupy a special status. When humans hear of a species that has become extinct, they are often saddened. When the species is one with which they are familiar, they are saddened even more, and they are especially concerned when an existent species is endangered by the expansion of society. For extinction of a species is not only a loss for science; it is the loss of an ancestor and the impoverishment of our experience. Hence the thought that a species as a whole, if not any given member of it, has an inherent right to be preserved as far as possible. But even here the strength of the interest that shapes the policy is less than absolute. There is no principle that absolutely requires humans to preserve a threatened species. But given our deep regret at the prospective loss, we are likely to demand preservation.

Appendix 1

Animal Consciousness

Ever since the time of Descartes, thinkers have risen
up to prove that animals do not have feelings. This
contention is so flagrant in its denial of common
sense that it seems sometimes to be merely perverse.
Descartes, to be sure, must be exempted from this
charge. He, at least, did not begin by looking for reasons to deny that animals have feelings and sensations. He was driven to that conclusion only by other
very serious philosophic problems. His reflections
on consciousness led him to conclude that the thinking mind and the external world were two completely
separate realms of existence. Sensations and feelings, on this assumption, could have no place to exist
other than in the thinking mind, and capacity to
think depended on the ability to use language.

Hence Descartes's principled move against animals. Since animals lack language, they cannot think;
since they cannot think, they cannot feel; and since
they cannot feel, they cannot have any sensations,
including even pain. Even higher animals other than
humans are automata whose motions, cries, and
gestures are simply the automatic responses of a
machine. We can therefore use them without concern
about any pain we might be causing them. For
Descartes, and especially for his "science-minded"

followers, it was now justifiable to carry on all manner of barbarous and hideous experiments. The animals might scream, but they supposedly felt nothing.

But if soul and body, mind and reality, were as completely separated as Descartes thought, how could even humans have any knowledge whatsoever of the external world? Given the purely mental genesis of all our sensations and images, it would seem that Descartes' theory of mind made all contact with the world impossible. The ultimate solution to this problem, within the framework of Cartesian dualism, was occasionalism in one form or another. The most prominent proposals were by Arnold Geulincx and Nicolas Malebranche, among others, who were two of Descartes's early followers. According to Malebranche, whose occasionalist doctrine is best known, the gap between the human mind and external reality is directly and immediately bridged by intervening acts of God. Every time we want to scratch our nose, God divines our intention and moves our hand.

This was a desperate solution and one might have thought that, faced with a difficulty this huge, Descartes might have relented on the inability of animals to feel. But he was, at least to some extent, driven and sustained by ideology. Descartes was a committed Catholic who could not admit that animals might go to heaven along with human beings. Given his dualism, that would follow if animals had consciousness at all.

That animals had psyches and were conscious had been no problem in official Catholic doctrine, as for example in St. Thomas and the Scholastics, because animal souls were subrational and could not be redeemed. Descartes' radical dualism, however, left no room for intermediate subrational psyches. Every soul, if it existed all, had to be of the same order. Either all of them were eligible for an afterlife, or none at all.

The radically dualistic part of Descartes's philosophy has long since been abandoned or greatly modified. The gap it opened is simply too great to be intelligibly explained. All the empirical evidence and scientific findings of biology are against it, to say nothing of ordinary common sense. The obvious structural similarity between animals and humans makes the uselessness ascribed to their sensory faculties absurd. And without real experience of pain, pleasure, and reproductive desire, the whole evolutionary process would become inexplicable.

Nevertheless, in the last twenty-five years there has been a neo-Cartesian revival in which an essentially Cartesian result—namely, that animals feel no pain—is achieved, allegedly by different and more reasonable means. I do not find that any of these theories are driven by serious philosophical necessity. In any case, all of them fail utterly, as I shall attempt to show in the four illustrations of neo-Cartesian arguments that follow:

1. The earliest, to my knowledge, is by R. G. Frey, who concedes that animals are conscious but denies they can have desires and beliefs.[1] Desires, he points out correctly, presuppose beliefs. I cannot desire something unless I have an idea of what I am after and believe that it will satisfy some interest of mine. But Frey contends that one cannot have a belief without language. Only with language can we frame a sentence that we can believe is true or false. If he is granted that much, Frey can readily go on to perfect his entire "case against animals." For he has now proven that they do not have desires.

Animal rights in the style of Regan would make no sense if animals have no desires, because in order to have a right to something one has to have an interest in it. And animals, Frey thinks he has shown, can have no interest in anything because they cannot desire anything. This is the main part of his case against animals. Once that is demonstrated, he seems willing to concede that animals might feel very simple pains. Frey, like Singer, is a utilitarian, so the pain of animals would have to be reckoned before we are free to make any given use of them. But Frey believes, as we have noted earlier, that the losses humans would suffer if they followed the path of vegetarianism would clearly offset the pain undergone by animals. He does not present us with any figures on the comparative harms and pleasures, and it is extremely doubtful he could do so given the endless billions of animals cruelly destroyed each year by humans. We are thus free to discard this part of his case as wishful thinking. The present issue in any event is whether animals can have desires and beliefs.

Frey offers a hypothetical case to illustrate his reasoning:

> Suppose I am a collector of rare books and desire to own a Gutenberg Bible: my desire to own this volume is to be traced to my belief that I do not now own such a work and that my collection is deficient in this regard. By "to be traced" here, what I mean is this: if someone were to ask how my belief that my collection lacks a Gutenberg Bible is connected with my desire to own such a Bible, what better or more direct reply could be given than that, without this belief, I would not have had this desire? For if I believed that my collection *did* contain a Gutenberg Bible and so was complete in this sense, then I would not desire such a Bible in order to make up what I now believe to be a notable deficiency in my collection. (Of course, I might desire to own more than one such Bible, but this contingency is not what is at issue here). (86–87)

He then goes on to conclude:

> If what is believed is that a certain sentence is true, then no creature which lacks language can have beliefs; and without beliefs, a creature cannot have desires. (88)

Unfortunately for Frey's argument, however, belief is needed not only for rare book collectors who want a Gutenberg Bible, but even for the simplest desires. I have noticed I am hungry and that I lack something sweet, cold, smooth, and preferably vanilla tasting. I realize that I lack a vanilla ice cream cone. But I cannot desire a cone without believing there is one out there to be had. Perhaps there is one over there in that luncheonette and perhaps it will satisfy my hunger. My dog, no doubt, cannot be aware that she lacks a Gutenberg Bible. But she can believe that she is lacking her evening meal and desire it. Frey may think of course that this sort of simple desire hardly counts. But if so he is begging the question. He will not consider those beliefs of animals or humans that do not fit his hypothesis that animals have no desires. And on this consideration alone his "case against animals" is lost.

This answer to Frey technically depends on showing that desires can exist without beliefs that depend on the ability to think through sentences. For a full account, I particularly recommend the precise and extended critique by Sapontzis.[2] But I think that for present purposes, I may stop with the previous reflection. One cannot have the simplest desire without belief, and if animals cannot have beliefs we go back almost all the way to Descartes. Frey would grant them "consciousness" but it turns out to be virtually empty. How can a being have a pain without desiring to get rid of it? If desire depends on belief, how can a being without language want to get rid of a pain at all?

Regan too refutes Frey effectively on somewhat different grounds, and on finishing with Frey he takes up Stephen Stich, who argues that animals have beliefs but that we cannot not know what they are.[3] This contention, although challenging theoretically, is less immediately relevant to the issue of animal rights than Frey's, and so I will not offer comments of my own or summarize Regan's. If my dog likes a certain kind of food for dinner, and is clearly appeased in her desire when I feed her that food, I need not worry whether her idea of food and mine are the same (even though I strongly suspect that there is considerable overlap).

2. Peter Harrison wishes "to show that Descartes's view of animal pain can seriously be entertained without the necessity of subscribing to Descartes's unfortunate ontology."[4] He begins with the thought that humans surely feel more pain than animals because humans are more highly evolved and more sensitive on many different levels. That much is hardly to be doubted. But Harrison then presses on to claim that animals do not feel pain at all. Wildebeests make no sound when being torn apart by predators. Hence there is no reason to believe any animal feels pain when being injured, their cries and gestures notwithstanding. Besides, there is no biological reason why animals *need* pain. Chimpanzees, for example, need help from other chimps when hurt, and *that* (not pain) may be why they

cry out. A hot iron causes a reflex of withdrawal when we put our finger on it, and the pain comes only afterward. Who needs the pain, then? Only humans do, thinks Harrison. They are higher animals, free to act *against* their reflexes. Hence they need a little pain here and there to warn them against being so free with that freedom that they will burn themselves badly. Even so, pain is not after all neural; it is psychic and you need a highly conscious human-style ego to feel it.

How, then, can animals have pain and not have it at the same time? This is a difficult question, but Harrison opines that animals do have pain but immediately forget it. There is no continuing identity in animals that allows them to be conscious of it. And now comes the master stroke. How, Harrison asks, can animals learn if they forget all pains? He turns for an answer to the humble protozoa. They do not even have a nervous system, and yet they learn! "I am not claiming here," says Harrison, "that all learning processes work in the same way as those of the *Protozoa*, but simply making the point that learning can take place without the requirement of consciousness" (138).

What, then, according to Harrison, is the great legacy that evolution has conferred on humans, the highest of all creatures and the only one capable of feeling pain? It is pain, and pain alone, that gives us dignity. "It is our capacity for pain which has given rise to those uniquely human attributes of courage, resignation, self-control, perseverance, endurance, and their opposites" (132). I will offer no further comment on this point, and I will not bother to provide obvious examples of such virtues among animals.

Harrison, however, will not leap to rash conclusions, and so he warns us that it is not yet certain that we may beat our young children and our pets with a clear conscience:

> It should not be thought that I am advocating that we beat our infants
> and pets. There are other moral considerations which show this kind
> of behavior to be wrong irrespective of what patients feel.   (138)

3. Peter Carruthers observes that he can drive his car and steer it correctly to his destination with his mind taken up by other things.[5]

His absorption elsewhere can be so deep that he does not remember and cannot recall how he drove. He is thus persuaded that there can be unconscious experiences. For humans, to be sure, only some experiences are unconscious. But Carruthers boldly suggests that *all* animal experiences are unfelt and unrecalled. The way now seems open to declare that animals do not feel pain.

Thus far, however, Carruthers' argument is extremely weak. The blackout of consciousness in driving a car is presumably a kind of hypnosis. I can hardly imagine it occurring when the road is dangerous and unfamiliar. Like the even more dangerous effect of falling asleep at the wheel, it is most likely caused by the monotonous repetition of the easy and familiar. Are we then to assume that all animals are in some sort of hypnotic trance?

Perhaps not. Carruthers next considers the phenomenon of blindsight. People who have suffered lesions in the striate cortex report that they cannot see and do not experience the sensation of vision, and yet they discern objects in their visual field. It is as though the visual field is not reported to the brain. And so Carruthers wonders whether animals can have vision that goes unreported for lack of consciousness!

But the argument now goes on to even deeper neurological reflections. Carruthers believes that "a conscious experience is a state whose content is available to be consciously thought about (that is, which is available for description in acts of thinking which are themselves available to further acts of thinking)" (263). What is needed to experience an experience is thus a second-order spontaneous consciousness of that experience, which doesn't always happen. It didn't happen when he drove the car, says Carruthers, and so it remained a nonconscious experience.

Animals have no second-order consciousness; they do not think. Carruthers suspects, but does not insist, that the reason they do not think is that they do not have language and cannot form sentences. In any event, pain is an experience that, like any other, has to be available to a second-order consciousness in order to be experienced.

A new difficulty now appears. The second-order consciousness, if one is to be conscious of that consciousness, must be available to a yet higher order of consciousness, and so on if we are to be conscious of *that* consciousness. But unless we keep on going up in levels, how will we ever have an idea of the thing that's out there that started the whole chain of second-order effects? We may close the gap perhaps, but in order to do so we may need a second Malebranche! God perhaps bestows a final consciousness of consciousness (on humans only, to be sure) and he does that every time we remember that we drove a car or scratched our nose.

In any event, as far as animals are concerned, Carruthers is satisfied that he has done the job:

> Similarly then in the case of brutes: since their experiences, including their pains, are nonconscious ones, their pains are of no immediate moral concern. Indeed, since all the mental states of brutes are nonconscious, their injuries are lacking even in indirect moral concern. Since the disappointments caused to a dog through possession of a broken leg are themselves nonconscious in their turn, they too are not appropriate objects of our sympathy. Hence, neither the pain of the broken leg itself, nor its further effects on the life of the dog, have any rational claim upon our sympathy. (268)

Animals, therefore, should not evoke our sympathy. It is a waste of effort that could be better spent. Babies, however, are a different story. They too lack conscious pain, says Carruthers, but for some reason not explained, the pains of which *they* are unconscious have an effect on the life of which they will become conscious later on! It is important, therefore, that

> they should continue to evoke our sympathy. For a baby's pains and injuries [which, of course, they cannot feel and will never be able to recall], are likely to have a significant effect upon the person the baby will one day become. (269)

4. The problem of animal pain is a deep and difficult issue in theology as well, and here the attempts at a solution are more interesting. We have already noted in chapter 5 the existence of a longstand-

ing minority tradition in Christianity that envisages the resurrection of animals. A powerful recent statement is by Stephen H. Webb:

> That animals are morally innocent does not mean that they do not need redemption, if redemption means deliverance from suffering. Only if the afterlife is imagined solely as a place of judgment does moral capability play such a determining role. What if heaven is not about reward and punishment but rather redemption and consolation? What if heaven allows for the completion of what is left incomplete in this life? Keith Ward has spoken eloquently about animal afterlife. "If there is any sentient being which suffers pain, that being—whatever it is and however it is manifested—must find that pain transfigured by a greater joy" (1974:223). Indeed, that justice demands an afterlife for those unable to make the best of their situation is the best reason to believe in an afterlife for humans as well.[6]

There are, however, some serious zoological problems with this point of view. C.S. Lewis famously questions whether animal resurrection is a coherent idea. He doubts the capacity of animals to experience genuine suffering, and concludes that they do not have, by nature, a sufficient consciousness of self to benefit from resurrection. He argues that lower animals such as a newt can feel pain but cannot be said to suffer because they cannot remember former pain or anticipate a future pain. Hence they do not have the kind of memory of their experiences that would enable them to profit from redemption. They would not recognize a resurrected self as their own:

> The real difficulty about supposing most animals to be immortal is that immortality has almost no meaning for a creature which is not 'conscious' in the sense above. If the life of a newt is merely a succession of sensations, what should we mean by saying that God may recall to life the newt that died to-day? It would not recognize itself as the same newt; the pleasant sensations of any other newt that lived after its death would be just as much, or just as little a recompense for its earthly sufferings (if any) as those of its resurrected—I was going to say 'self', but the whole point is that the newt probably has no self.[7]

Lewis is agnostic about self-consciousness even in higher animals. Elephants, even in the wild, presumably have some form of self-consciousness and so a "rudimentary" individuality. But for the most part he would limit resurrection to those higher animals who have been tamed and loved by humans. The ideal example here would be the faithful and well-treated sheepdog. Such animals acquire a sense of identity from their quasi-membership in a family.

This position does not deny that animals feel pain, but only that most of them lack a sufficient sense of identity to be recompensed for pain by resurrection. This, I believe, does not effectively provide theology with an acceptable theodicy of animal pain. It does not explain how a loving God can have created sentient beings who suffer pain and death without possibility of compensation. That is not our problem here, however. For present purposes the important issue is Lewis's view of animal identity.

I do not believe that very simple forms of life, like newts, can lack all memory of the sensations that occur in them. I cannot imagine any biological function of pain (or pleasure) unless it is remembered, at least for a short time. For it is pain and pleasure that steer even the simplest sentient creatures. If these sensations are completely without function, we are back once again with Descartes's paradoxes. And Lewis would surely have agreed that animals, if they can remember sensations at all, must have some sort of self.

Appendix 2

Biomedical Testing and
Use of Animals

To inflict death or pain on animals for scientific or medical research is wrong morally, and ought to be prohibited. This follows from everything said in the text about the rights of animals. This does not mean that animals may never be deliberately harmed or become subjects of research. They may be killed in order to protect the health of humans (and other animals) if they are infected with a serious disease and cannot be quarantined. They may be used in benign research such as teaching chimpanzees to understand and use sign language. But even when the purpose of research is to benefit the animals themselves, inflicting pain or death in the process of research is wrong. Animals cannot give consent. Hence, unlike humans, they cannot be called upon to sacrifice even for the good of other animals.

Medical practitioners and scientific researchers protest that to outlaw animal research would deal a severe blow to medical and scientific progress. Their argument is at best overstated. The use of animals in biomedical research and practice is often unnecessary even on existing assumptions:

1. Much of it is frivolous, as in cosmetics testing, or is mere routine, as when researchers "test" for the

public relations advantage of being able to say they "tested"; or is utterly useless, as in tests designed to confirm what is obvious or already known; or all too often cynical, as in the call for tests to pry funds out of the government or to get tenure for assistant professors in a hurry.

2. Much of it is counterproductive. Tests on animals often give false negatives when the substance in question would actually benefit humans, as with polio vaccines. Even more often, testing is positively harmful, as in the negative results obtained in thalidomide and lung cancer tests, and the misleading results of in many drug tests.

3. There are alternatives that can supplant animal testing if people are willing to spend the extra funds to develop them. These include electronic and computer modeling, animal tissue testing, epidemiological research, and stem cell experimentation.

4. Human mortality and morbidity rates would be more quickly reduced if only a portion of the funds now spent on exotic animal research were rerouted to public health measures, especially in the Third World and developing countries.

No doubt, claims made either for or against the value of animal testing cannot be accurately measured. The helpfulness for science of most tests is hard to determine and can rarely be quantified. In other words, one cannot be sure whether biomedical knowledge would have progressed more quickly or more slowly—later or sooner—had there been no tests on animals. By the same token, neither can we know whether biomedical science might not have been more advanced had it not relied on animal testing and gone down alternative paths.

This is not to say that the use of animal products is not important in contemporary medical practice. Vaccines, tests for the effects of drugs on individuals, and the like may require painful uses of animals. Even more dramatically, lifesaving operations may use parts of animals as substitutes for human organs. A human has a bad heart and is about to die. To save that patient, new valves or an entire heart must be transplanted from a pig or a cow.

Should we allow the patient to die in the name of animal rights? Suppose you have a sick child or spouse whose heart is about to fail. Only animal transplants are available, and the parts needed are right at hand in the hospital freezer. Since the loved one is too ill to be consulted, it is up to you decide for or against the transplant. What would you choose?

The morally correct answer is to decline the transplant. You cannot escape by pleading a conflict of rights between animal and human. It is not as though *both* the spouse and the animal must die if you do not choose one or the other to be saved. That the animal, in our example, is already dead does not really make a difference. It was perfectly healthy and would have lived but for deliberate human execution. If you decide to use the organ of this animal, another will be killed to restock the refrigerator.

The agony of the person forced to make the decision is perhaps some excuse if he or she should overrule conscience in the particular case. One has to acknowledge the overwhelming temptation the individual facing bereavement would feel by doing what current public law permits and what medical science expects and advocates. But whoever yields to this temptation should know that he or she is doing wrong and be prepared to make amends. That person is under a special obligation to press for legislation outlawing the practice of animal transplants in the future. That would not be inconsistent. The temptation in any given situation may be terribly cruel and ought to be put beyond our choice. Suppose, however, the hypothetical case is our own—that our heart is bad and we must decide for or against an animal transplant for ourselves. Here the excuse for saying yes is weaker, and the obligation to push for removing individual temptation by law even more solemn, if that is possible.

To press for such a public law, furthermore, need not cause medical science to give up on transplants. Such a law would divert even more efforts of research to produce artificial vital organs, and might even lead to more lasting successes in the treatment. New hearts, new valves, and the like, ought to be, and increasingly are, made from nonsentient materials.

Science and medicine can thus progress without exploiting animals.

The line of development may be different. The rate of advance may be slowed. The choice of drugs or modes of surgery may have to be tested on a few human volunteers rather than numerous animals, and knowledge of effects may often depend on sheer trial and error with human patients. The price for humans is therefore likely to be high, although probably not nearly as high as conservatives believe. But high or low, the gain in human decency and general respect for life makes the risk worthwhile.

Notes

Preface

1. The term "animals" will always refer to nonhuman animals unless otherwise specified.

1. Peter Singer and Utilitarianism

1. Technically speaking, utilitarians do not recognize rights outside or beyond those created and imposed by positive legislation. This is why Singer uses the term "animal liberation" rather than animal rights to indicate his doctrine of equal respect for animal interests.
2. As the following quotation indicates, utilitarians sometimes use the term "rights" loosely. Strictly speaking, all rights for them are the consequence of legislation. Technically, no rights are natural. But the language of rights is sometimes convenient for utilitarians in order to express the principle that all sentient entities must have their interests considered in a calculation of aggregate utility.
3. Bentham, *An Introduction to The Principles of Morals and Legislation*, 311n. Here and throughout all emphases are in the original unless otherwise noted.
4. Singer, *Animal Liberation*, chs. 2–4.
5. See also Gary L. Francione's list of objections with extended answers in the appendix to his *Introduction to Animals Rights: Your Child or the Dog?* (Francione is emphatically not a utilitarian).
6. Frey, *Utility and Rights*, 19.
7. Frey, *Rights, Killing, and Suffering*, 28–29.
8. Ibid., 198ff.

9. Singer, *Practical Ethics*, 181ff.
10. A point denied by Singer, in *Practical Ethics*, 95.
11. Singer, *Animal Liberation*, 85ff.
12. Singer, *Animal Liberation*, 81ff. See also Singer, *Practical Ethics*, 75ff.

2. Regan on Animal Rights

1. Among others, see especially Frey, *Interests and Rights*, and Stich, "Do Animals Have Beliefs?" See also Harrison, "Theodicy and Animal Pain," and Carruthers, "Brute Experience." See appendix 2 for commentary on these authors' statements.
2. Regan, *The Case for Animal Rights*, 1–82.
3. See Francione, *Introduction to Animal Rights*, 138.
4. Regan, *The Case for Animal Rights*, 150.
5. On Narveson see below. I do not discuss him specifically here since his view is based on enlightened egoism rather than the demands of reason.
6. Regan, The Case for Animal Rights, 187.
7. Francione, *Introduction to Animal Rights*, 138.
8. Regan, The Case for Animal Rights, 246.
9. Peter Carruthers, *The Animals Issue*, 22–23.
10. Pluhar, in *Beyond Prejudice*, writes, "Moral patients cannot do what is right or wrong, as we have said, and in this respect they differ fundamentally from moral agents. But moral patients can be on the receiving end of the right and wrong acts of moral agents, and so in this respect resemble moral agents. A brutal beating administered to a child, for example, is wrong, even if the child herself can do no wrong. . . . Moral patients can do nothing right or wrong that affects or involves moral agents, but moral agents can do what is right or wrong in ways that affect or involve moral patients" (154).
11. Regan also defends the "argument from marginal cases" in his "Narveson on Egoism and the Rights of Animals," 179–186.
12. The phrase was first used in Narveson, "Animal Rights," 164. Narveson makes the same move that Pluhar says is still open to those who deny that animals have rights. "Infants and morons" are no better off than animals; morality "covers" them in the same way it does animals—that is, indirectly, by the effect of their suffering on the feelings of proper humans (177).
13. Pluhar, *Beyond Prejudice*, 177–178.
14. Regan, *Defending Animal Rights*, 13.
15. Francione, *Introduction to Animal Rights*, chap. 3.

3. Animal Rights and Kant

3. Animal Rights and Kant

1. Not all Kant commentators hold to this. It may be claimed that the first form of the categorical imperative, taken by itself, is simply indeterminate (see below). But see O'Neill, "Consistency in Action," 120–121.
2. Pogge, "The Categorical Imperative," 200.
3. "As a sentient being I am sensitive to suffering and pain, and so cannot reasonably will the permission to confine or kill me. Therefore, I cannot reasonably will universal legislation permitting that any sentient being be confined or killed, and thus (by universality) must not adopt a maxim pursuant to which any sentient being can be confined or killed" (197). Pogge goes on to observe: "For better or worse, this is not an argument Kant would accept. Universalizations are to range over the domain of rational beings only."
4. Pogge reads FH as excluding animals, for he applies it not only to all humans but to humans only. He holds that rational beings "alone, objectively, are ultimate sources of value or ends in themselves" (197).
5. See also Regan, *The Case for Animal Rights*, 184–185.
6. Kant, *Groundwork of the Metaphysic of Morals*, 96 [428], and "Duties to Animals and Spirits," 239–241. For the *Groundwork*, page numbers in brackets refer to the German edition of Kant's collected works by the Prussian Royal Academy.
7. Kant, *Critique of Judgment*, First Introduction, 20:236, quoted in Kemp, *The Philosophy of Kant*, 113.
8. Kant, "Duties to Animals and Spirits," 239–240.
9. *The Summa contra Gentiles of Saint Thomas Aquinas*, book 3, part 2, chaps. 84–163, specifically chap. 112:92; and *Summa Theologiae*, vol. 29, Ia2ae.102,6, 225.
10. See generally Sorabji, *Animal Minds and Human Morals*.
11. Broadie and Pybus, "Kant and the Maltreatment of Animals," 560. Surprisingly, Regan's *Animal Rights* (180–181) disagrees with Broadie and Pybus on the grounds that maltreatment could have meant for Kant merely making something unfit for efficient human use, which would apply also to spoiling an inanimate instrument. But surely what Kant had in mind was not spoiling but causing suffering.
12. Nozick, *Anarchy, State, and Utopia*, 36.
13. Kant, *Groundwork of the Metaphysics of Morals*, 96 [429].
14. Paul Guyer proposes to interpret FH as an obligation to preserve ethical

131

reason (in the sense of FUL) and to promote it in others. See Guyer, "The Possibility of the Categorical Imperative," 233. But it is hard to see why "preserve" and "promote" should be more than empirical ends.

15. Pogge, "The Categorical Imperative," 197–198.

16. Ibid., 198.

17. Wood, *Kant's Ethical Thought*,124.

18. Paul Guyer, on the other hand, who also argues for the priority of FH in interpreting the categorical imperative, may leave the door open for a broader view of the scope of the categorical imperative. He holds that "any particular exercise of rational nature is itself an instance of that which is absolutely good and yet also has an aim that is outside of and larger than itself" (233).

19. See the quotation from Pogge in note 3, above.

20. The question as to what sort of entities can have rights also arises in jurisprudence. In "Rights" (115ff.), McCloskey denies that animals can have rights in any juridical sense. The foundation of the opposing view is discussed in Feinberg, "The Nature and Value of Rights" (243ff.). The actual and potential legal standing of animals in American law and jurisprudence is debated by a number of contributors to Cass Sunstein and Martha Nussbaum, eds., *Animal Rights* (Oxford: Oxford University Press, 2004).

21. Regan, "Feinberg on What Sorts of Beings Can Have Rights," 497.

22. Kant, *Groundwork*, 106–107 [439].

23. For a critique of such conceptions as actually used, see Francione, *Animals, Property, and the Law*, especially chap. 3.

24. "Kindness" to animals could be considered an "imperfect obligation" in that, like our duty to be charitable (as distinct from being just), it is not owed to any creature in particular and so does not correspond to any claim right in those who might benefit from an act of kindness or of charity. (See, for example, O'Neill, *Constructions of Reason*, 140 and 189ff.) But cruelty to animals is a wholly different matter. Acts of cruelty will almost always be directed against specific animal(s), and are therefore unjust. Any intuition that it is prima facie wrong to harm an animal indicates that animals have rights. This is not to say, however, that there are no (imperfect) duties toward animals. We owe them kindness and where institutions are established by the government—let us say to remove abandoned animals from the street in a humane manner—we may have, indirectly, a perfect obligation of support—e.g., by paying taxes.

25. On this last point see Regan, *The Case for Animal Rights*, 297ff; and Franklin, "Regan on the Lifeboat Problem: A Defense," 189–201.

26. Regan, *The Case for Animal Rights*, 239.
27. Gewirth, *Reason and Morality*, 104–105.
28. Ibid., 134–135. See also 201–202.
29. Pluhar, *Beyond Prejudice*, 261.

4. Animal Rights and Post-Kantian Rationalism

1. Rawls, *A Theory of Justice*, 505.
2. Ibid., 512.
3. See Regan, *The Case for Animal Rights*, 165ff.
4. Regan takes up, and criticizes, what Rawls may have meant by an indirect duty to animals, and does so thoroughly and at considerable length. See Regan's *The Case for Animal Rights*, 163ff. Owing to the ambiguity of some key statements of Rawls, the line between his view of indirect duty and his reasons for excluding animals from the original position is sometimes difficult to draw. Regan thus touches from time to time on difficulties in Rawls's basic position. Some of Regan's objections on this score will be evident from quotations given below. I have not pursued the issue of indirect duties as it bears on Rawls. I have already indicated why I believe that no such theory can work. And once again, I would note that the line separating direct and indirect duty in Rawls is uncertain.
5. Regan, *The Case for Animal Rights*, 294–297.
6. Rawls, *A Theory of Justice*, 505.
7. Ibid., 509.
8. Ibid., 510. See also Rawls, *Political Liberalism*, 25–34.
9. Regan in *The Case for Animal Rights* (167–168) seems to believe that the natural duties are independent, but my colleague Robert Amdur has persuaded me that they are not. According to Amdur they are simply dispositions to be just.
10. See Regan, *The Case for Animal Rights*, 167.
11. Ibid., 512. Neither animals, defectives, nor charity are mentioned in *Political Liberalism*.
12. Rawls, *Political Liberalism*, lecture 4, no. 5.
13. Ibid., 151–152, 157.
14. Regan, *The Case for Animal Rights*, 171.
15. Ibid., 173–174. See also Donald Van de Veer, "Of Beasts, Persons, and the Original Position," 368–377.
16. Rawls, *Political Liberalism*, 27.
17. Carruthers, *The Animals Issue*, 102. See also Donald Van de Veer, "Of

Beasts, Persons, and the Original Position," 368–377, and Robert Elliot, "Rawlsian Justice and Non-Human Animals," 95–106.

18. Van de Veer, "Of Beasts, Persons, and the Original Position," 375–376.

19. Carruthers, *The Animals Issue*, 102–103.

20. Habermas, *Moral Consciousness and Communicative Action*, 65–66.

21. Ibid., 88–89.

22. Outhwaite, *Habermas: A Critical Exposition*, 45.

23. Habermas, Moral Consciousness and Communicative Action, 138.

24. O'Neill, *Constructions of Reason*, 23.

25. Rousseau, *Emile*, 118–120.

26. Diderot, "Droit Naturel," *Encyclopédie*, 115–116 (translation mine).

27. See Hume, *An Inquiry Concerning the Principles of Morals*, 21.

28. See Narveson, "Animal Rights," 161–178. This article is a critical review essay of various articles and books by Regan and by Singer.

29. See Regan's reply to Narveson in the same issue: Regan, "Narveson on Egoism and Rights of Animals," 179–186. This critique of Narveson is recapitulated in Regan, *The Case for Animal Rights*, 156ff.

30. Carruthers, *The Animals Issue*, 102–103.

31. As though doubtful that this argument will do the job, Carruthers offers the thought that animals really are not aware of the pain they feel. This is one of a number of neo-Cartesian reflections on animal awareness that I shall take up in an appendix.

32. The argument is developed at length by Pufendorf in reply to Grotius, *On the Law of War and Peace*, book 1, chap. 1, par. 10. See Samuel Pufendorf, *On the Law of Nature and Nations*, edition of 1688, book 2, chap. 3. Further aspects of the debate between intellectalists and voluntarists, which was widespread in this period, are briefly summarized in chapter 1 of Haakonssen, *Natural Law and Moral Philosophy*. Locke's position is not as immediately evident as Pufendorf's but is substantially the same even in Locke's early reflections on natural law. See Ward, "Divine Will, Natural Law, and the Voluntarism/Intellectualism Debate in Locke," 208–218.

33. Locke, *Two Treatises of Government*, the *Second Treatise*, par. 4.

5. Animal Rights and Compassion

1. Kant, *Groundwork*, 61 [393].

2. Schweitzer, *Civilization and Ethics*, 246.

3. Donovan, "Animal Rights and Feminist Theory," 34–59.

4. See especially Adams, "Woman-Battering and Harm to Animals," 55–84, but the entire collection is worth investigation.
5. Donovan, "Animal Rights and Feminist Theory," 41ff.
6. Ibid., 45.
7. Gilligan, *In a Different Voice*, 29.
8. Donovan, "Attention to Suffering: Sympathy as a Basis for Ethical Treatment of Animals," 147–169.
9. Claudia Card takes a broadly similar position in "Particular Justice and General Care," 99–106. See especially page 100: "The view of justice as imposing scruples and of care as setting goals could account for a common view, to which Professor Held objects, that justice and care are compatible in the following way: once the requirements of justice are met, we are permitted to act on considerations of care. This view may seem to reduce care ethics to matters of personal preference, optional deeds. Yet, one could understand care as imposing requirements also, but requirements that do not come into play until general duties of justice are satisfied. This appears to be Kant's understanding. His duty to help others is presented as 'imperfect.' Imperfect duties, he says, must always yield to perfect ones in cases of conflict between them, and duties of justice are perfect." In this passage Card is commenting on Virginia Held, "Caring Relations and Principles of Justice," in Sterba, 67–81.
10. Donovan, "Attention to Suffering," 52.
11. Francione, "Ecofeminism and Animal Rights," 96. Francione advances a general critique of welfareism in animal rights organizations in his book *Rain Without Thunder, the Ideology of the Animal Rights Movement*.
12. Kant, *The Metaphysics of Morals*, 198.
13. Regan, *The Thee Generation*, 3.
14. Kook, *The Lights of Penitence*, 317ff.
15. Irenaeus, *Against Heresies*, in *The Ante-Nicene Fathers*, vol. 1, 563.
16. Linzey, *Animal Theology*, 100ff.
17. Webb, *On God and Dogs*, 174ff.
18. One among many expressions of this prophecy in the Qur'an is Surah 6:38, in *The Meaning of the Holy Qur'an*, 303:

There is not an animal
(That lives) on the earth,
Nor a being that flies
On its wings, but (forms
Part of) communities like you.

Nothing have we omitted
From the Book, and they (all)
Shall be gathered to their Lord
In the end.

19. On the Ebionites and other early vegetarian Christian sects, see Akers, *The Lost Religion of Jesus*, and Tomson and Lambers-Petry (eds.), *The Image of Judeo-Christians in Ancient Jewish and Christian Literature*.

20. I do not in this context take up natural theologies or metaphysical systems supportive of animal rights. I have therefore not considered Daniel A. Dombrowski's attempt to develop the idea of respect for animals from the holism of Charles Hartshorne and Alfred North Whitehead. See Dombrowski, *Hartshorne and the Metaphysics of Animal Rights*.

21. There are many such stories. This one appears in Pandit, *Transcendence and Negation*, 129–130.

6. Conflict of Rights and Environmentalism

1. Regan, *The Case for Animal Rights*, 285–286.

2. I ignore a third option—which is to draw lots for all five occupants. But that only complicates the argument without changing the basic issue.

3. The following discussion of the lifeboat case is a restatement, with only minor changes, of my argument in "Regan on the Lifeboat Problem: A Defense," 189–201.

4. Peter Singer, "Ten Years of Animal Liberation," 50.

5. Jamieson, "Rights, Justice, and Duties to Provide Assistance," 349–362.

6. Regan, *The Case for Animal Rights*, 305.

7. Singer, "Ten Years of Animal Liberation," 50.

8. Regan and Singer, "The Dog in the Lifeboat," 57.

9. But see this volume, ooo.

10. Singer, "Ten Years of Animal Liberation," 50.

11. Regan and Singer, "The Dog in the Lifeboat," 57.

12. Singer, "Ten Years of Animal Liberation," 49.

13. Francione, "Comparable Harm and Equal Inherent Value," 87.

14. Nagel, *Mortal Questions*, 169.

15. Peter Singer has attempted to show that it might be possible to compare the value of our own lives with those of animals in *Practical Ethics*, 88–90. There is also a far-reaching rejection of Nagel's denial of our capacity to imagine the lives of other species in Coetzee, *The Lives of Animals*, 31ff.

Appendix 1: Animal Consciousness

16. Pluhar, *Beyond Prejudice*, 291–292.
17. Singer, *Practical Ethics*, 106.
18. Sapontzis, *Morals, Reason, and Animals*, 81.
19. Francione, "Comparable Harm and Equal Inherent Value," 85.
20. Regan, *The Case for Animal Rights*, 233–234.
21. Ibid., 362–363.
22. Callicott, "Animal Liberation: A Triangular Affair," 56.
23. Callicott, "Animal Liberation and Enviromental Ethics: Back Together Again," 257.
24. Callicott, *Beyond the Land Ethic*, 147.
25. Ibid., 73
26. Taylor, *Magpies, Monkeys, and Morals*, 129.

Appendix 1. Animal Consciousness

1. Frey, *Interests and Rights: The Case Against Animals*.
2. Sapontzis, *Morals, Reason, and Animals*, 115–129.
3. Regan, *The Case for Animal Rights*, 49–61.
4. Harrison, "Theodicy and Animal Pain," 128.
5. Carruthers, "Brute Experience," 258–269.
6. Webb, *On God and Dogs*, 175.
7. Lewis, *The Problem of Pain*, 125.

Bibliography

Adams, Carol J. "Woman-Battering and Harm to Animals." In *Animals and Women*, edited by Carol J. Adams and Josephine Donovan, 55–84. Durham and London: Duke University Press, 1995.

Akers, Keith. *The Lost Religion of Jesus*. New York: Lantern Books, 2000.

Aquinas, Thomas. *The Summa contra Gentiles of Saint Thomas Aquinas*. Literally translated by the Dominican Fathers from the latest Leonine Edition. London: Burns, Oates, and Washburn Ltd., 1973–1979.

———. *Summa Theologiae*. Vol. 29. Translated by David Bourke and Arthur Littledale. Westminster: Blackfriars, 1969.

Bentham, Jeremy. *An Introduction to The Principles of Morals and Legislation*. New York: Hafner Publishing Company, 1948.

Broadie, Alexander, and Elizabeth M. Pybus. "Kant and the Maltreatment of Animals." *Philosophy* 53 (1978): 560–561.

Callicott, J. Baird. "Animal Liberation: A Triangular Affair." In *The Animal Rights / Environmental Ethics Debate*, edited by Eugene C. Hargrove, 37–69. Albany: State University of New York Press, 1992.

———. "Animal liberation and enviromental ethics: Back together again." In *The Animal Rights / Environmental Ethics Debate*, edited by Eugene C. Hargrove, 249–261. Albany: State University of New York Press, 1992.

———. *Beyond the Land Ethic: More Essays in Environmental Philosophy*. Albany: State University of New York Press, 1999.

Card, Claudia. "Particular Justice and General Care." In *Controversies in Feminism*, edited by James P. Sterba, 99–106. Lanham, Maryland: Rowman and Littlefield, 2001.

Carruthers, Peter. "Brute Experience." *The Journal of Philsophy* 86, no. 5 (May 1989): 258–269.

———. *The Animals Issue*. Cambridge: Cambridge University Press, 1992.

Coetzee, J. M. *The Lives of Animals*. Princeton: Princeton University Press, 1999.

Cohen, Carl, and Tom Regan. *The Animal Rights Debate*. Lanham, Maryland: Rowman and Littlefield, 2001.

Diderot, Denis. "Droit Naturel," *Encyclopédie*, t.v. 115–116. Reprinted in *The Political Writings of Jean Jacques Rousseau*, by C. E. Vaughan, 429–433. New York: John Wiley and Sons, 1962.

Dombrowski, Daniel A. *Hartshorne and the Metaphysics of Animal Rights*. Albany: State University of New York Press, 1988.

Donovan, Josephine. "Attention to Suffering: Sympathy as a Basis for the Ethical Treatment of Animals." In *Animals and Women*, edited by Carol J. Adams and Josephine Donovan, 147–169. Durham and London: Duke University Press, 1995.

——. "Animal Rights and Feminist Theory." In *Beyond Animal Rights: A Feminist Caring Ethic for the Treatment of Animals*, edited by Josephine Donovan and Carol J. Adams, 34–59. New York: Continuum Press, 1996.

Elliot, Robert. "Rawlsian Justice and Non-Human Animals." *Journal of Applied Philosophy* 1, no. 1 (1984): 95–106.

Feinberg, Joel. "The Nature and Value of Rights." *The Journal of Value Inquiry* 14, no. 4 (Winter, 1970): 243–257.

Francione, Gary L. *Animals, Property, and the Law*. Philadelphia: Temple University Press, 1995.

——. "Comparable Harm and Equal Inherent Value: The Problem of the Dog in the Lifeboat." *Between the Species* (Summer and Fall, 1995): 81–89.

——. *Rain Without Thunder, the Ideology of the Animal Rights Movement*. Philadelphia: Temple University Press, 1996.

——. "Ecofeminism and Animal Rights: A Review of *Beyond Animal Rights: A Feminist Caring Ethic for the Treatment of Animals*." *Women's Rights Law Reporter* 18, no. 1 (Fall 1996): 95–106.

——. *Introduction to Animal Rights: Your Child or the Dog?* Philadelphia: Temple University Press, 2000.

Franklin, Julian H. "Regan on the Lifeboat Problem: A Defense." *Environmental Ethics* 23 (Summer 2001): 189–201.

Frey, Raymond G. *Interests and Rights: The Case Against Animals*. Oxford: Clarendon Press, 1980.

——. *Rights, Killing, and Suffering: Moral Vegetarianism and Applied Ethics*. Oxford: Basil Blackwell, 1983.

——. *Utility and Rights*. Oxford: Basil Blackwell, 1985.

Gewirth, Alan. *Reason and Morality*. Chicago: University of Chicago Press, 1978.

Gilligan, Carol. *In a Different Voice*. Cambridge: Harvard University Press, 1993.

Guyer, Paul. "The Possibility of the Categorical Imperative." In *Kant's Groundwork of the Metaphysics of Morals*, edited by Paul Guyer, 215–246. Maryland: Rowman and Littlefield, 1998.

Haakonssen, Knud. *Natural Law and Moral Philosophy*. Cambridge: Cambridge University Press, 1996.

Habermas, Jürgen. *Moral Consciousness and Communicative Action*. Translated by Christian Lenhardt and Shierry Weber Nicholsen. Cambridge, Massachussets: The MIT Press, 1991.

Harrison, Peter. "Theodicy and Animal Pain." *Philosophy* 64, no. 247 (January 1989): 79–92, reprinted in *Animal Experimentation: The Moral Issues*, edited by Robert M. Baird and Stuart E. Rosenbaum, 128–139. Buffalo: Prometheus Press, 1991.

Held, Virginia. "Caring Relations and Principles of Justice." In *Controversies in Feminism*, edited by James P. Sterba, 67–81. Lanham, Maryland: Rowman and Littlefield, 2001.

Irenaeus. "Against Heresies." In *The Ante-Nicene Fathers*, vol. 1, edited by Alexander Roberts and James Donaldson, 309–567. Grand Rapids, Mich.: Eerdmans, 1950.

Jamieson, Dale. "Rights, Justice, and Duties to Provide Assistance: A Critique of Regan's Theory of Rights." *Ethics* 100 (January 1990): 349–62.

Kant, Immanuel. *Groundwork of the Metaphysic of Morals*. Translated and edited by H.J. Paton. New York: Harper, 1964.

——. "Duties to Animals and Spirits." In *Lectures on Ethics*, edited by Peter Heath and J. B. Schneewind, translated by Peter Heath, 212–213. Cambridge: Cambridge University Press, 1997.

——. *Critique of Judgment*. Translated by James Creed Meredith. Oxford: Clarendon Press, 1952.

——. *The Metaphysics of Morals*. Translated by Mary Gregor. Cambridge: Cambridge University Press, 1996.

Kemp, John. *The Philosophy of Kant*. London: Oxford University Press, 1968.

Kook, Abraham Isaac. *The Lights of Penitence, Lights of Holiness, The Moral Principles, Essays, Letters, and Poems*. Translated by Ben Zion Bokser. New York: Ramsey, 1978.

Lewis, C. S. *The Problem of Pain*. London: Centenary Press, 1940.

Linzey, Andrew. *Animal Theology*. Urbana and Chicago: University of Illinois Press, 1995.

Locke, John. *Two Treatises of Government*. Cambridge: Cambridge University Press, 1988.

McCloskey, H. J. "Rights." *The Philosophical Quarterly* 15, no. 59 (April 1965): 115–127.

Nagel, Thomas. *Mortal Questions*. New York: Cambridge University Press, 1979.

Narveson, Jan. "Animal Rights." *Canadian Journal of Philosophy* 7, no. 1 (March 1987): 161–178.

Nozick, Robert. *Anarchy, State, and Utopia*. New York: Basic Books, 1974.

O'Neill, Onora. "Consistency in Action." In *Kant's Groundwork of the Metaphysics of Morals*, edited by Paul Guyer, 103–132. Lanham, Maryland: Rowman and Littlefield, 1998.

———. *Constructions of Reason: Explorations of Kant's Practical Philosophy*. Cambridge: Cambridge University Press, 1989.

Outhwaite, William. *Habermas: A Critical Exposition*. Stanford: Stanford University Press, 1994.

Pandit, Moti Lal. *Transcendence and Negation: A Study of Buddhist Compassion and Christian Love*. New Delhi, 1999.

Pluhar, Evelyn B. *Beyond Prejudice: The Moral Significance of Human and Nonhuman Animals*. Durham and London: Duke University Press, 1995.

Pogge, Thomas. "The Categorical Imperative." In *Kant's Groundwork of the Metaphysics of Morals*, edited by Paul Guyer, 189–213. Maryland: Rowman and Littlefield, 1998.

Qur'an. *The Meaning of the Holy Qur'an* (text, translation, and commentary). 10th ed. Beltsville, Maryland: Amana Publications, 1999.

Rawls, John. *A Theory of Justice*. Cambridge: Harvard University Press, 1971.

———. *Political Liberalism*. New York: Columbia University Press, 1993.

———. *The Law of Peoples*. Cambridge: Harvard University Press, 1999.

———. *Justice as Fairness*. Cambridge: Harvard University Press, 2001.

Regan, Tom. "Feinberg on What Sorts of Beings Can Have Rights." *The Southern Journal of Philosophy* 14, no. 4 (1974): 485–498.

———. "Narveson on Egoism and the Rights of Animals." *Canadian Journal of Philosophy* 7, no.1 (March 1977): 179–186.

———. *All that Dwell Therein: Animal Rights and Environmental Ethics*. Berkeley: University of California Press, 1982.

———. *The Case for Animal Rights*. Berkeley: University of California Press, 1983.

———. *The Thee Generation: Reflections on the Coming Revolution*. Philadelphia: Temple University Press, 1991.

———. *Defending Animal Rights*. Urbana and Chicago: University of Illinois Press, 2001.

Regan, Tom, and Peter Singer. "The Dog in the Lifeboat." *The New York Review of Books*, 25 April 1985, 57.

Bibliography

Rousseau, Jean Jacques. *Emile*. Translated by Barbara Foxley. London: J. M. Dent and Sons, 1982.

Sapontzis, S. F. *Morals, Reason, and Animals*. Philadelphia: Temple University Press, 1987.

Schweitzer, Albert. *Civilization and Ethics*. London: A. and C. Black, 1929.

Singer, Peter. "Ten Years of Animal Liberation." *New York Review of Books*, January 17, 1985, 50.

———. *Animal Liberation*. New York: Avon Books, 1990.

———. *Practical Ethics*. Cambridge: Cambridge University Press, 1993.

Sorabji, Richard. *Animal Minds and Human Morals: The Origins of the Western Debate*. Ithaca, N.Y.: Cornell University Press, 1993.

Sunstein, Cass R., and Martha Nussbaum, eds. *Animal Rights*, Oxford: Oxford University Press, 2004.

Taylor, Angus. *Magpies, Monkeys, and Morals: What Philosophers Say about Animal Liberation*. Ontario: Broadview Press, 1999.

Tomson, Peter and Doris Lambers-Petry, eds. *The Image of Judaeo-Christians in Ancient Jewish and Christian Literature*. Tübingen: Mohr, 2003.

Van de Veer, Donald. "Of Beasts, Persons, and the Original Position." *The Monist* 62, no. 3 (July 1979): 368–377.

Ward, W. Randall. "Divine Will, Natural Law, and the Voluntarism/Intellectualism Debate in Locke." *History of Political Thought* 16, no. 2 (Summer 1995): 208–218.

Webb, Stephen H. *On God and Dogs*. New York: Oxford, 1998.

Wood, Allen W. *Kant's Ethical Thought*. Cambridge: Cambridge University Press, 1999.

Index

Index

Index

justice, 10, 53, 75, 135n. 9; abstract, 80, 85; act utilitarianism and, 7–8; distributive, 59–60, 61, 62; ethic of care and, 81–83; formal, 18–19, 21; limits of theory of, 54–55; political, 57–58, 61

Kant, Immanuel: on action and moral worth, 77–78; antifoundationalist interpretation of, 65–66; exclusion of animals from moral standing, 19, 22–23, 34, 36, 51–52; on indirect duty, 36–37; on perfection, 41; on rational beings, 40. *See also* categorical imperative
Kook, Abraham, 86

land ethic, 106–10
language, consciousness and, 115, 117–19, 121
Leopold, Aldo, 106–7, 109
Lewis, C.S., 123–24
lifeboat case, 91–94; applied to environmentalism, 106, 110–11; as automatic priority for humans, 102–5; as exceptional, 98–99, 105; utilitarian view, 95–97; worse-off principle, 95–96, 104
life expectancies, 101–2
lifesaving operations, 126–27
lifeworld, 64–65
Locke, John, 71–74
love, 85

Malebranche, Nicolas, 116
marginal cases, argument from, 26–28, 55–56. *See also* infant examples; mental deficiency arguments

maxims, 43; antisocial, 34–35; discursive method and, 63–65; legitimate, 32–34; restrictions, 32–33
mental deficiency arguments, 9–10, 11, 25–26, 55–57
Metaphysics of Morals, The (Kant), 71, 85
mine disaster case, 95, 97
miniride principle, 95, 97
mixed community, 108
moral agents, 14; duty not to harm, 16–17; formula of universal law and, 32–34; inherent value of, 17–20; opportunities for satisfaction, 92–93, 96–97; rational beings as, 35. *See also* rational beings
morality, source of, 24–25
moral patients, 31, 130n. 10; duty not to harm, 14–18; formula of sentience applied to, 35–36, 42–43; human, rights of, 55–56; human intervention on behalf of, 61–62; inherent value of, 17–20, 94
moral persons, 54–56
moral pluralism, 109

Nagel, Thomas, 100
Narveson, Jan, xiii, 14, 15, 69, 130n. 12
natural duties, 56, 133n. 9
nature: right to, 89–90; state of, 51, 71–72; state of equality, 72–73; values as nonexistent in, 23–24
neo-Cartesianism, xiv, 13, 117; Carruthers, 120–22; Frey, 117–19; Harrison, 119–20
Nietzsche, Friedrich, 103, 104
Nozick, Robert, 38

occasionalism, 116

O'Neill, Onora, 65–67, 68

"On the Duty of Love to Other Human Beings" (Kant), 85

original position, 14, 53–55; animals included in, 58–60; difference principal, 59–60, 62; exclusion of animals from, 54–58; revision of, 60–61

Outhwaite, William, 64

pain: infants and, 122; as necessity for humans, 119–20; utilitarian view, 2, 6–7, 10–11

perfectionism, 18–19, 21, 41, 45–46, 103–4

Pluhar, Evelyn B., xiii, 25–28, 130n. 10; on animal satisfaction, 100–101; rationalist moral theory of, 27–28, 48–50

pluralism, moral, 109

Pogge, Thomas, 32–35, 42–43, 131nn. 3, 4

political constructivism, 57–58

political justice, 53, 57–58, 61

Political Justice (Rawls), 58

Political Liberalism (Rawls), 57, 59

practical discourse, 64

Practical Ethics (Singer), 101

practical reason, 77–78

preference utilitarianism, 9–10

prereflective intuition, 47–48, 92

prevention cases: automatic priority for humans, 102–5; deliberate action, 94, 97–98; equal inherent value, 92–93; as exceptional, 98–99, 105; life expectancies, 101–2; mine disaster case, 95, 97; miniride principle, 95, 97; worse-

off principle, 95–96, 104. *See also* lifeboat case

prima facie duty, 16–17, 20, 24

principal of generic consistency (PGC), 49–51

private right, 71

property, 28, 83–84, 90

protection, 42, 74

prudentialism, 75

public right, 71

Pybus, Elizabeth M., 37, 131n. 11

Qur'an, 87, 135–36n. 18

rational beings, 19, 35, 40, 43–44. *See also* moral agents

rationalist moral theory, 31; of Gewirth, xiii, 48–51; of Pluhar, xiii, 25–28, 48–50, 100–101, 130n. 10

rationality, xii–xiii, 19

Rawls, John, xiii, 14–15, 51, 70; indirect duty to animals, 54–55, 133n. 4; justice concept, 53–58, 61. *See also* original position

reason: practical, 77–78; rules of, 79–80

reasonableness, 70

reflective intuition, 24–25, 47–48, 93

Regan, Tom, xii, xiv, 10, 133n. 4; aggregate utility, rejection of, 15–16; on animal consciousness, 13–14; animal experimentation, view of, 97–99; Carruthers's critique of, 23–25, 69; duty, view of, 14–15; ecofeminist view of, 80–81, 84–86; environmental issues and, 91–97; Francione's critique of, 102–5; harm principal, 16–17, 22;

Index

utilitarianism, xi–xii, 75, 117, 129nn.
1, 2; act utilitarianism, 7–8; common sense *vs*., 5–7; death, view of,
4, 9; equal inherent value and,
93–94; fairness and, 7–8, 62; flaws
in doctrine, 5–6; pain and pleasure, view of, 2, 6–7, 10–11; preference utilitarianism, 9–10; prevention cases and, 95–97; Regan's
view, 14, 21; responsibility of
meat-eater, 3–4; rule utilitarianism, 7–8; Singer's view, 2–3,
8–11
utility, aggregate, 5–6, 8, 11, 15–16,
95–96
utility indices, 5–7

values, as nonexistent in natural
world, 23–24. *See also* inherent
value
vegetarianism, 4–5, 10–11, 117
veil of ignorance, 53–54, 59

Webb, Stephen H., 123
welfareism, 84
"What Is It Like to Be a Bat?" (Nagel),
100
wild animals, 62, 108, 112
will: ends of, 39; formal principles
of, 39; formula of autonomy, 47;
formula of the kingdom of ends,
46–47; general, xiii, 67–68; of
God, 71–73; good will, 77–78
will-to-live, 79
Wood, Allen, 43–44
worse-off principle, 95–96, 104